PRIMARY MATHEMATICS 4A

TEXTBOOK

Marshall Cavendish
Education

Original edition published under the title Primary Mathematics Textbook 4A

© 1982 Curriculum Planning & Development Division

Ministry of Education, Singapore

Published by Times Media Private Limited

This American Edition

© 2003 Times Media Private Limited

© 2003 Marshall Cavendish International (Singapore) Private Limited

© 2014 Marshall Cavendish Education Pte Ltd

Published by Marshall Cavendish Education

Times Centre, 1 New Industrial Road, Singapore 536196

Customer Service Hotline: (65) 6213 9688

US Office Tel: (1-914) 332 8888 | Fax: (1-914) 332 8882

E-mail: cs@mceducation.com

Website: www.mceducation.com

First published 2003

Reprinted 2003

Second impression 2004

Reprinted 2004, 2005 (twice), 2006 (thrice), 2007 (twice), 2008,
2009 (twice), 2010 (twice), 2011, 2012, 2014, 2015, 2016,
2017, 2018 (twice), 2019 (twice), 2020 (twice), 2021

ISBN 978-981-01-8506-0

Printed in Singapore

ACKNOWLEDGEMENTS

Our special thanks to Richard Askey, Professor of Mathematics (University of Wisconsin,
Madison), Yoram Sagher, Professor of Mathematics (University of Illinois, Chicago), and Madge
Goldman, President (Gabriella and Paul Rosenbaum Foundation), for their indispensable
advice and suggestions in the production of Primary Mathematics (U.S. Edition).

PREFACE

Primary Mathematics (U.S. Edition) comprises textbooks and workbooks. The main feature of this package is the use of the **Concrete ➡ Pictorial ➡ Abstract** approach. The students are provided with the necessary learning experiences beginning with the concrete and pictorial stages, followed by the abstract stage to enable them to learn mathematics meaningfully. This package encourages active thinking processes, communication of mathematical ideas and problem solving.

The textbook comprises 7 units. Each unit is divided into parts: ❶, ❷, . . . Each part starts with a meaningful situation for communication and is followed by specific learning tasks numbered 1, 2, . . . The textbook is accompanied by a workbook. The sign $\boxed{\text{Workbook Exercise}}\!>$ is used to link the textbook to the workbook exercises.

Practice exercises are designed to provide the students with further practice after they have done the relevant workbook exercises. Review exercises are provided for cumulative reviews of concepts and skills. All the practice exercises and review exercises are optional exercises.

The color patch ■ is used to invite active participation from the students and to facilitate oral discussion. The students are advised not to write on the color patches.

CONTENTS

Whole Numbers

1 Numbers to 100,000

 **One dollar**

 **Ten dollars**

 **One hundred dollars**

 **One thousand dollars**

 **Ten thousand dollars**

How much money is there altogether?

$20,000

Twenty thousand dollars

$3000

Three thousand dollars

$500

Five hundred dollars

$40

Forty dollars

$8

Eight dollars

The total amount of money is $23,548.

$23,548

Twenty-three thousand, five hundred forty-eight dollars

Ten thousands	Thousands	Hundreds	Tens	Ones
10000 10000	1000 1000 1000	100 100 100 100 100	10 10 10 10	1 1 1 1 1 1 1 1
2	3	5	4	8

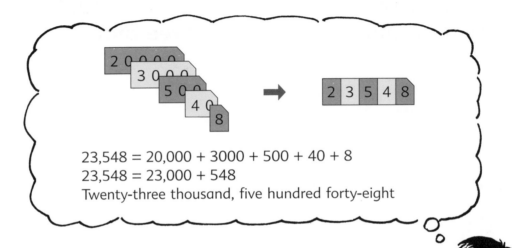

23,548 = 20,000 + 3000 + 500 + 40 + 8
23,548 = 23,000 + 548
Twenty-three thousand, five hundred forty-eight

1. Read and write the following in words.
    (a) 2753   (b) 7919   (c) 4908
    (d) 3056   (e) 7280   (f) 5002
    (g) 27,165   (h) 18,057   (i) 42,605
    (j) 30,003   (k) 60,109   (l) 81,900

2. Write the following in figures.
    (a) Eight thousand, twelve
    (b) Forty-nine thousand, five hundred one
    (c) Seventeen thousand, four
    (d) Ninety thousand, ninety

Workbook Exercise 1

3. What are the missing numbers?

5000	6000	7000				
					20,000	
29,500	29,600	29,700				30,100
			28,800			
24,230						
24,130			26,800		60,000	
24,030					70,000	
			24,800			
23,830	23,820	23,810				23,770
23,630		23,650		23,670		23,690

4. Use place-value cards to make a **5-digit number** like this:

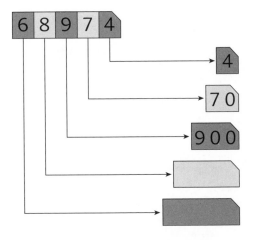

In 68,974, the digit **8** stands for ■ and the digit **6** stands for ■.

5. What does the digit **8** stand for in each of the following 5-digit numbers?

(a) 16,**8**14 (b) **8**2,114 (c) 4**8**,050

Workbook Exercise 2

9

6. (a) Count the ten thousands, thousands, hundreds, tens and ones in this chart.

Ten thousands	Thousands	Hundreds	Tens	Ones
10000 10000 10000	1000 1000 1000 1000 1000	100 100	10 10 10 10 10 10	

(b) What number is represented by the set of number discs?
(c) Which digit is in the hundreds place?
(d) Which digit is in the ten thousands place?
(e) What is the value of each digit in the number?

7. 26,345 people watched a soccer game at a stadium.

(a) Use a set of number discs to represent 26,345.
(b) 26,345 is ■ more than 26,000.
(c) 26,345 is ■ more than 6345.

8. What number does each letter represent?

(a)

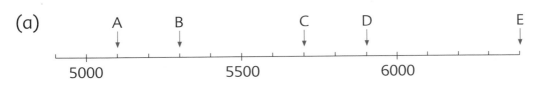

(b)

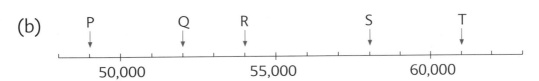

9. (a) Which number is smaller, 56,700 or 75,600?

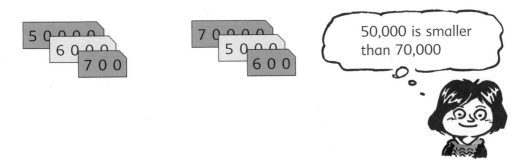

(b) Which number is greater, 32,645 or 32,498?

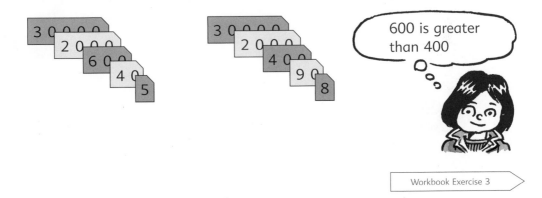

Workbook Exercise 3

10. Find the value of
    (a) 6000 + 8000
    (b) 27,000 + 4000
    (c) 15,000 − 6000
    (d) 31,000 − 5000
    (e) 7000 × 4
    (f) 10,000 × 5
    (g) 12,000 ÷ 3
    (h) 30,000 ÷ 6

Workbook Exercise 4

② Rounding Off Numbers

Our Savings

Maggie	$61
Rosa	$68
Brandy	$75

Maggie: I save about $60.

Rosa: I save about $70.

Brandy: I save about $80.

They **round off** each of the numbers 61, 68 and 75 to the nearest ten.

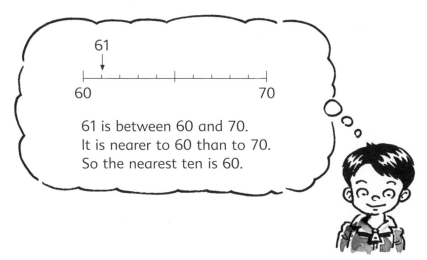

61 is 60 when rounded off to the nearest ten.

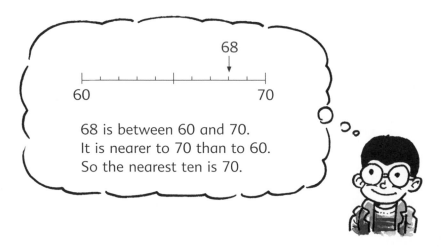

68 is 70 when rounded off to the nearest ten.

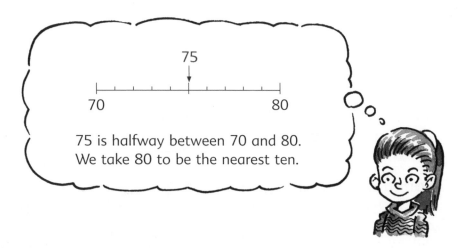

75 is 80 when rounded off to the nearest ten.

1. Round off each number to the nearest ten.
    (a) 29   (b) 38   (c) 82   (d) 95

2. Round off each number to the nearest ten.
    (a) 234

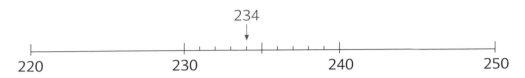

    234 is between 230 and 240.
    234 is nearer to 230 than to 240.
    234 is ■ when rounded off to the nearest ten.

    (b) 1458

    1458 is between 1450 and 1460.
    1458 is nearer to 1460 than to 1450.
    1458 is ■ when rounded off to the nearest ten.

    (c) 2735

    2735 is halfway between 2730 and 2740.
    2735 is ■ when rounded off to the nearest ten.

3. Round off each number to the nearest ten.
    (a) 129   (b) 201   (c) 452   (d) 685
    (e) 2069   (f) 4355   (g) 4805   (h) 5508

Workbook Exercise 5

4. There are 2478 students in Lakeview School.
    (a) Round off the number of students to the nearest ten.

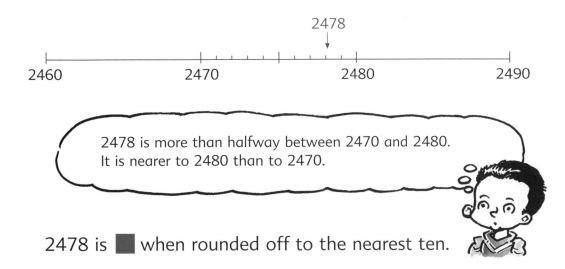

    2478 is more than halfway between 2470 and 2480.
    It is nearer to 2480 than to 2470.

    2478 is ■ when rounded off to the nearest ten.

    (b) Round off the number of students to the nearest hundred.

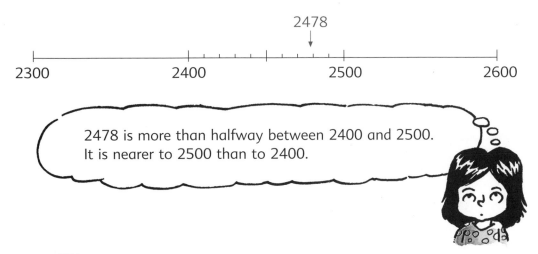

    2478 is more than halfway between 2400 and 2500.
    It is nearer to 2500 than to 2400.

    2478 is ■ when rounded off to the nearest hundred.

5. Mr. Ricci sold his car for $34,125.
    Round off this amount to the nearest $100.

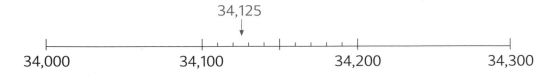

    $34,125 is $■ when rounded off to the nearest $100.

6. Round off each number to the nearest hundred.

   (a) 345

   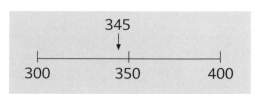

   (b) 3670

   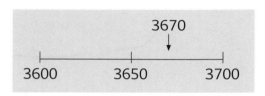

   (c) 4850

   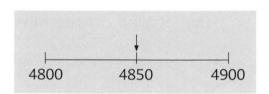

   (d) 27,050

   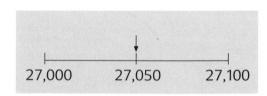

   (e) 42,629

   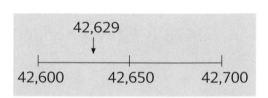

7. Round off each number to the nearest hundred.
   (a) 320   (b) 486   (c) 650   (d) 980
   (e) 2915   (f) 3075   (g) 4308   (h) 5150
   (i) 14,234   (j) 25,520   (k) 32,450   (l) 52,090

   Workbook Exercise 6

8. Round off each number to the nearest hundred.
Then **estimate** the value of 712 + 492.

$$712 \longrightarrow 700$$
$$492 \longrightarrow 500$$

700 + 500 =

The value of 712 + 492 is about ■.

9. Round off each number to the nearest hundred.
Then estimate the value of
(a) 384 + 296   (b) 507 + 892   (c) 914 + 707
(d) 716 − 382   (e) 983 − 296   (f) 1408 − 693

10. Estimate the value of 786 − 297 + 518.

Round off each number
to the nearest hundred.
$$786 \longrightarrow 800$$
$$297 \longrightarrow 300$$
$$518 \longrightarrow 500$$

800 − 300 + 500 = ■

The value of 786 − 297 + 518 is about ■.

11. Estimate the value of
(a) 418 + 293 + 108   (b) 784 + 617 + 399
(c) 814 + 208 − 587   (d) 1205 − 489 − 596

Workbook Exercise 7

17

PRACTICE 1A

1. Write the following in figures.
   (a) Twelve thousand, eight hundred three
   (b) Twenty thousand, fifty
   (c) Seventy thousand

2. Write the following in words.
   (a) 1758   (b) 5306   (c) 72,903   (d) 91,120

3. What is the value of the digit **6** in each of the following?
   (a) 54,0**6**0   (b) 34,**6**20   (c) **6**0,143   (d) 27,00**6**

4. Complete the following number patterns.

   (a) 5780, 5880, ■, ■, 6180
   (b) 32,465, 33,465, ■, ■, 36,465
   (c) 53,700, 63,700, 73,700, ■, ■

5. Arrange the numbers in increasing order.
   (a) 30,601, 30,061, 30,160, 30,016
   (b) 29,999, 90,000, 20,990, 29,909

6. Round off each number to the nearest ten.
   (a) 89   (b) 725   (c) 4621   (d) 9099

7. Round off each number to the nearest hundred.
   (a) 837   (b) 15,468   (c) 39,963   (d) 46,050

8. Round off each number to the nearest hundred and then estimate the value of
   (a) 576 + 329   (b) 2154 + 887
   (c) 3948 + 208   (d) 682 − 207
   (e) 7078 − 238   (f) 5402 − 179
   (g) 2590 + 109 − 484   (h) 1368 − 919 − 289

3 Factors

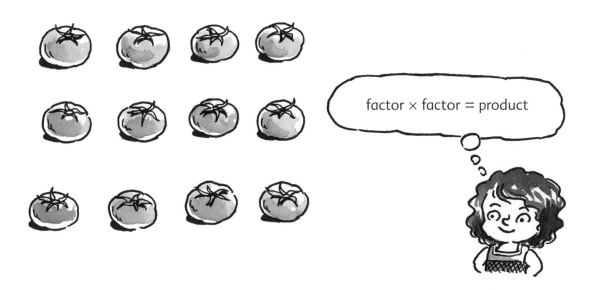

factor × factor = product

$$3 \times 4 = 12$$

12 is the **product** of 3 and 4.
3 and 4 are **factors** of 12.

$$2 \times 3 \times 4 = 24$$

24 is the **product** of 2, 3 and 4.
2, 3 and 4 are **factors** of 24.

1.
 $1 \times 6 = 6$

$2 \times 3 = 6$

We can write a number as a product of two factors in different ways.

1, 2, ▉ and ▉ are factors of 6.

Is 4 a factor of 6?

Is 5 a factor of 6?

2.

$2 \times 8 = 16$

2 and 8 are factors of 16.

Name other factors of 16.

3. Find the factors of each number.
   (a) 7   (b) 9   (c) 10   (d) 18

4. (a) Which of the following numbers have 2 as a factor?
       8,   10,   15,   24

   (b) Which of the following numbers have 5 as a factor?
       15,   20,   25,   32

Workbook Exercise 8

5. (a) Is 3 a factor of 21?

$$\begin{array}{r} 7 \\ 3\overline{)21} \\ 21 \\ \hline 0 \end{array}$$

21 can be divided by 3 exactly.
So 3 is a factor of 21.

(b) Is 3 a factor of 26?

$$\begin{array}{r} 8 \\ 3\overline{)26} \\ 24 \\ \hline 2 \end{array}$$

26 cannot be divided by 3 exactly.
So 3 is not a factor of 26.

6. (a) Is 2 a factor of 98?
   (b) Is 4 a factor of 98?

7. (a) Is 4 a factor of 60?
   (b) Is 4 a factor of 84?
   (c) Is 4 a common factor of 60 and 84?

8. (a) Is 5 a common factor of 75 and 80?
   (b) Is 8 a common factor of 72 and 96?

9. Find the missing factors.
   (a) $28 = 7 \times$ ■
   (b) $40 = 5 \times$ ■
   (c) $72 = 8 \times$ ■
   (d) $81 = 9 \times$ ■
   (e) $63 = 9 \times$ ■
   (f) $56 = 7 \times$ ■

10. Find the factors of 32.

$32 = 1 \times 32$
$32 = 2 \times 16$
$32 = 4 \times 8$

The factors of 32 are 1, 2, ■, ■, ■ and ■.

11. Find the factors of 48.

$48 = 1 \times 48$

$48 = 2 \times$ ■

$48 = 3 \times$ ■

$48 = 4 \times$ ■

$48 = 6 \times$ ■

The factors of 48 are 1, 2, 3, 4, 6, ■, ■, ■, ■ and 48.

12. Find the factors of 100.

$100 = 1 \times 100$
$= 2 \times 50$
$= 4 \times 25$
$= \ldots$

13. Find the factors of each number.
   (a) 40   (b) 50   (c) 75   (d) 80

Workbook Exercise 9

4 Multiples

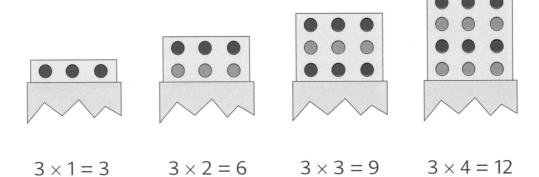

$3 \times 1 = 3$ $3 \times 2 = 6$ $3 \times 3 = 9$ $3 \times 4 = 12$

3, 6, 9 and 12 are **multiples** of 3.

The multiples of 3 have 3 as a factor.

9 is a multiple of 3.
3 is a factor of 9.

12 is a multiple of 3.
3 is a factor of 12.

Name other multiples of 3.

1. (a) Is 3 a factor of 36?
   (b) Is 36 a multiple of 3?

$$\begin{array}{r} 12 \\ 3{\overline{\smash{\big)}\,36}} \\ \underline{3} \\ 6 \\ \underline{6} \\ 0 \end{array}$$

$3 \times 12 = 36$

2. (a) Is 3 a factor of 23?
   (b) Is 23 a multiple of 3?

3. (a) Is 12 a multiple of 2?
   (b) Is 12 a multiple of 3?
   (c) Is 12 a multiple of 4?
   (d) Is 12 a multiple of 5?
   (e) Is 12 a multiple of 6?

4. List the first four multiples of 5.

$5 \times 1 = 5$
$5 \times 2 = 10$
$5 \times 3 = 15$
$5 \times 4 = 20$

5. List the first four multiples of 9.

6. Find the next three numbers in each of the following number patterns.

   (a) 4, 8, 12, 16, ■, ■, ■

   (b) 6, 12, 18, 24, ■, ■, ■

7. In the table below, the multiples of 2 are circled and the multiples of 5 are crossed.

1	(2)	3	(4)	X̶	(6)	7	(8)	9	(1̶0̶)
11	(12)	13	(14)	1̶5̶	(16)	17	(18)	19	(2̶0̶)
21	(22)	23	(24)	2̶5̶	(26)	27	(28)	29	(3̶0̶)
31	(32)	33	(34)	3̶5̶	(36)	37	(38)	39	(4̶0̶)
41	(42)	43	(44)	4̶5̶	(46)	47	(48)	49	(5̶0̶)
51	(52)	53	(54)	5̶5̶	(56)	57	(58)	59	(6̶0̶)
61	(62)	63	(64)	6̶5̶	(66)	67	(68)	69	(7̶0̶)
71	(72)	73	(74)	7̶5̶	(76)	77	(78)	79	(8̶0̶)
81	(82)	83	(84)	8̶5̶	(86)	87	(88)	89	(9̶0̶)
91	(92)	93	(94)	9̶5̶	(96)	97	(98)	99	(1̶0̶0̶)

(a) When a number is a multiple of 2, its ones digit is 0, 2, ■, ■ or ■.

(b) When a number is a multiple of 5, its ones digit is ■ or ■.

8. Write any number that is a multiple of 3.
    Find the sum of the digits of the number.
    Is the sum a multiple of 3?

25

9. The multiples of 4 are
   4, 8, **12**, 16, 20, 24, 28, . . .

   The multiples of 6 are
   6, **12**, 18, 24, 30, 36, 42, . . .

   12 is a **common multiple** of 4 and 6.

   Name the next two common multiples of 4 and 6.

There are more than one common multiple of 4 and 6.

10. (a) Which of the following numbers are common factors of 36 and 63?

   | 3 | 4 | 6 | 9 | 12 |

   (b) Which of the following numbers are common multiples of 6 and 9?

   | 9 | 18 | 27 | 36 | 45 |

11. Find a common multiple of 3 and 5.

The multiples of 5 are
5, 10, 15, 20, . . .
15 is also a multiple of 3.

Workbook Exercise 10

PRACTICE 1B

1. Write down all the factors of 18.

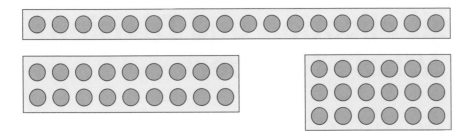

2. (a) Write down the next two multiples of 3.

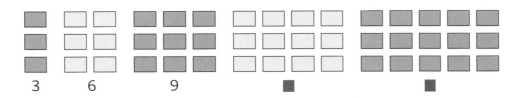

3   6   9

(b) Write down the next four multiples of 5.

0   5   10   15   20

3. Find the missing factors.

(a) $4 \times \blacksquare = 36$ (b) $6 \times \blacksquare = 54$

(c) $\blacksquare \times 8 = 56$ (d) $\blacksquare \times 9 = 27$

4. Find the factors of each number.

(a) 8   (b) 15   (c) 20

(d) 50   (e) 75   (f) 98

5. Find a common factor of each pair of numbers.

(a) 15 and 6   (b) 12 and 16   (c) 15 and 18

6. List the first four multiples of each number.

(a) 2   (b) 6   (c) 8

7. Find a common multiple of each set of numbers.

(a) 3 and 4   (b) 4 and 5   (c) 4 and 6

Multiplication and Division of Whole Numbers

1 Multiplication by a 1-digit Number, Division by a 1-digit Number and by 10

Sean has 1135 U.S. stamps.
He has 3 times as many foreign stamps as U.S. stamps.
(a) How many stamps does he have altogether?

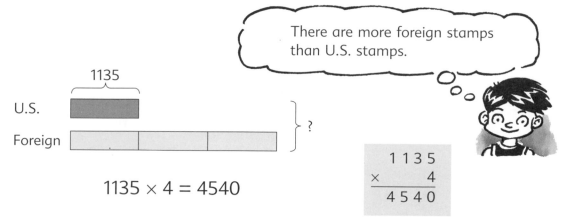

There are more foreign stamps than U.S. stamps.

$$1135 \times 4 = 4540$$

$$\begin{array}{r} 1135 \\ \times \quad 4 \\ \hline 4540 \end{array}$$

He has 4540 stamps altogether.

Multiply 1135 by 4.

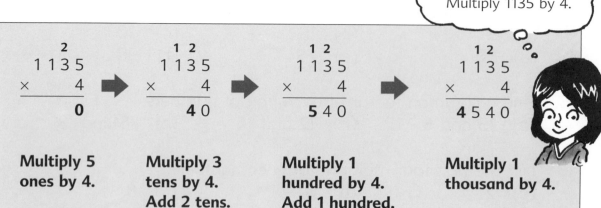

$$\begin{array}{r} {\scriptstyle 2} \\ 1135 \\ \times \quad 4 \\ \hline 0 \end{array} \Rightarrow \begin{array}{r} {\scriptstyle 12} \\ 1135 \\ \times \quad 4 \\ \hline 40 \end{array} \Rightarrow \begin{array}{r} {\scriptstyle 12} \\ 1135 \\ \times \quad 4 \\ \hline 540 \end{array} \Rightarrow \begin{array}{r} {\scriptstyle 12} \\ 1135 \\ \times \quad 4 \\ \hline 4540 \end{array}$$

Multiply 5 ones by 4.

Multiply 3 tens by 4. Add 2 tens.

Multiply 1 hundred by 4. Add 1 hundred.

Multiply 1 thousand by 4.

When 1135 is multiplied by 4, the **product** is 4540.

(b) If Sean puts the stamps equally into 5 packets, how many stamps are there in each packet?

$$4540 \div 5 = 908$$

```
      9 0 8
  5)4 5 4 0
    4 5
    ___
        4 0
        4 0
        ___
          0
```

There are 908 stamps in each packet.

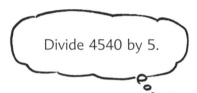

Divide 4540 by 5.

```
      9
  5)4 5 4 0
    4 5
```

➡

```
      9 0
  5)4 5 4 0
    4 5
    ___
        4
```

➡

```
      9 0 8
  5)4 5 4 0
    4 5
    ___
        4 0
        4 0
        ___
          0
```

Divide 45 hundreds by 5.

Divide 4 tens by 5.

Divide 40 ones by 5.

When 4540 is divided by 5, the **quotient** is 908 and the **remainder** is 0.

1. Multiply 3726 by 5.

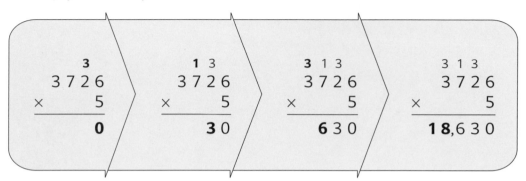

2. Multiply.
    (a) $2950 \times 6 = $ ■
    (b) $8 \times 3245 = $ ■

$$
\begin{array}{r}
2950 \\
\times \quad 6 \\
\hline
\end{array}
$$
■

$$
\begin{array}{r}
3245 \\
\times \quad 8 \\
\hline
\end{array}
$$
■

3. Estimate the value of 6218×4.

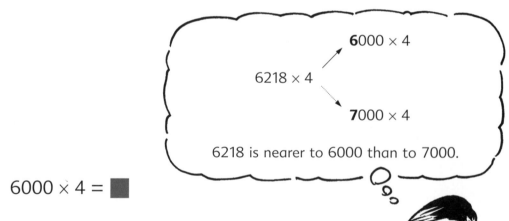

6218 × 4
6000 × 4
7000 × 4
6218 is nearer to 6000 than to 7000.

$6000 \times 4 = $ ■

The value of 6218×4 is about ■.

4. Estimate and then multiply.
    (a) 4076×5
    (b) 4317×8
    (c) 2050×9
    (d) 7×6931
    (e) 9×2173
    (f) 6×3840

Workbook Exercise 11

5. Divide 4206 by 3.

```
      1              1 4            1 4 0          1 4 0 2
  3)4 2 0 6      3)4 2 0 6      3)4 2 0 6      3)4 2 0 6
    3              3              3              3
  ———            ———            ———            ———
    1             1 2            1 2            1 2
                  1 2            1 2            1 2
                 ———            ———            ———
                                                  6
                                                  6
                                                ———
                                                  0
```

6. Divide.
   (a) 3250 ÷ 5 = ◼

   (b) 4235 ÷ 7 = ◼

   5)3250

   7)4235

7. (a) 40 ÷ 10 = ◼

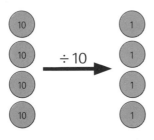

   (b) 400 ÷ 10 = ◼

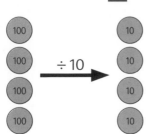

(c) $440 \div 10 =$ ■

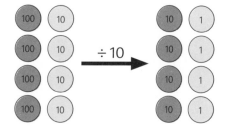

(d) $4440 \div 10 =$ ■

8. Estimate the value of $3840 \div 6$.

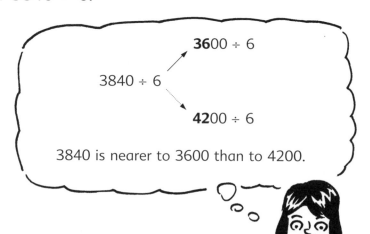

$3600 \div 6 =$ ■

The value of $3840 \div 6$ is about ■.

9. Divide 3245 by 10.

$$
\begin{array}{r}
3 \\
10\overline{)3245} \\
30 \\
\hline
2
\end{array}
\qquad
\begin{array}{r}
32 \\
10\overline{)3245} \\
30 \\
\hline
24 \\
20 \\
\hline
4
\end{array}
\qquad
\begin{array}{r}
324 \\
10\overline{)3245} \\
30 \\
\hline
24 \\
20 \\
\hline
45 \\
40 \\
\hline
5
\end{array}
$$

Workbook Exercise 12

10. Estimate and then divide.
    (a) 3604 ÷ 9   (b) 3580 ÷ 7   (c) 3120 ÷ 8
    (d) 8128 ÷ 10   (e) 7528 ÷ 3   (f) 7180 ÷ 6

11. The number of cars is 4 times the number of motorcycles in a town.
    (a) If there are 4356 cars, how many motorcycles are there?

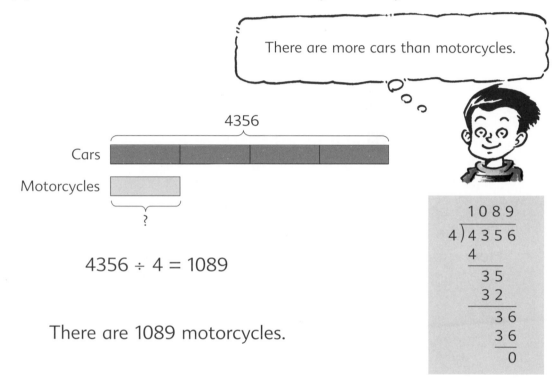

There are more cars than motorcycles.

4356 ÷ 4 = 1089

There are 1089 motorcycles.

```
      1 0 8 9
  4 ) 4 3 5 6
      4
      ─
      3 5
      3 2
      ───
        3 6
        3 6
        ───
          0
```

(b) How many cars and motorcycles are there altogether?

Method 1:

4356 + 1089 = ■

There are ■ cars and motorcycles altogether.

Method 2:

1089 × 5 = ■

There are ■ cars and motorcycles altogether.

12. Mr. Cohen earns $2935 a month.
If he spends $1780 each month and saves the rest, how much
will he save in 6 months?

> First, I find the amount
> Mr. Cohen saves each month.

$2935 - 1780 = 1155$

He saves $1155 each month.

$1155 \times 6 = $

He will save $ in 6 months.

13. David bought 6 cameras at $1340 each.
Then he bought another 8 cameras at $1248 each.
How much money did he spend altogether?

> First, I find the total amount
> David spent on the first 6 cameras
> and the total amount he spent on
> the next 8 cameras.

$1340 \times 6 = 8040$

He spent 8040 on the first 6 cameras.

$1248 \times 8 = 9984$

He spent 9984 on the next 8 cameras.

$8040 + 9984 = $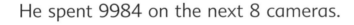

He spent $ altogether.

Workbook Exercise 13

PRACTICE 2A

Find the value of each of the following:

	(a)	(b)	(c)
1.	3 × 2011	4 × 2107	3450 × 5
2.	6 × 4215	3917 × 7	6258 × 9
3.	2109 ÷ 3	4036 ÷ 4	2510 ÷ 5
4.	7212 ÷ 6	3968 ÷ 8	8181 ÷ 9
5.	6431 ÷ 7	4750 ÷ 10	3299 ÷ 10

6. A baker sold 1380 cakes last month.
   He sold 3 times as many cakes this month as last month.
   How many cakes did he sell this month?

7. The cost of a computer is 4 times the cost of a printer.
   If the computer costs $2560, find the cost of the printer.

8. Josh had 1536 rubber bands.
   He put them equally into 6 boxes.
   How many rubber bands were there in each box?

9. James bought 3750 kg of rice. He packed the rice
   in bags of 10 kg each.
   How many bags of rice did he have?

10. The total cost of a scooter and 2 motorcycles is $9798.
    The cost of each motorcycle is $3654.
    Find the cost of the scooter.

11. For the last 4 months, Jake's monthly salary was $1895.
    He saved $3032 during the 4 months and spent the rest.
    How much did he spend?

② Multiplication by a 2-digit Number

$$32 \times 10 = 320 \qquad 320 \times 2 = 640$$

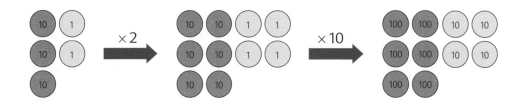

$$32 \times 2 = 64 \qquad 64 \times 10 = 640$$

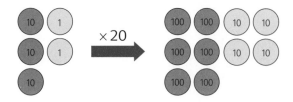

$$32 \times 20 = 640$$

1. Multiply.
   (a) 16×10
   (b) 40×10
   (c) 254×10
   (d) 10×29
   (e) 10×96
   (f) 10×380

2. Find the product of 14 and 30.

Method 1:

$$14 \times 30 = 14 \times 10 \times 3$$
$$= 140 \times 3$$
$$= \blacksquare$$

Method 2:

$$14 \times 30 = 14 \times 3 \times 10$$
$$= 42 \times 10$$
$$= \blacksquare$$

Method 3:

$$14 \times 3 = 42$$
$$14 \times 3\mathbf{0} = 42\mathbf{0}$$

3. Multiply.
   (a) $284 \times 20 = \blacksquare$

   $$\begin{array}{r} 284 \\ \times\quad 20 \\ \hline 568\mathbf{0} \end{array}$$

   (b) $40 \times 309 = \blacksquare$

   $$\begin{array}{r} 309 \\ \times\quad 40 \\ \hline 12{,}36\mathbf{0} \end{array}$$

4. Multiply.
   (a) 23×30 (b) 68×70 (c) 392×80
   (d) 50×36 (e) 90×45 (f) 560×60

Workbook Exercise 14

5. Multiply 34 by 15.

   $34 \times 15 = \blacksquare$

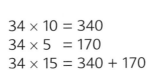

   $34 \times 10 = 340$
   $34 \times 5 \ = 170$
   $34 \times 15 = 340 + 170$

```
    3 4          3 4          3 4
  ×  1 5       ×  1 5       ×  1 5
  ───────      ───────      ───────
    1 7 0        1 7 0        1 7 0
                 3 4 0        3 4 0
                            ───────
                              5 1 0
```

6. Multiply.
   (a) $64 \times 27 = \blacksquare$

```
        6 4
     ×  2 7
     ───────
        4 4 8   ⟵  64 × 7
      1 2 8 0   ⟵  64 × 20
     ───────
      1 7 2 8
```

38

(b) $19 \times 278 = $

$$
\begin{array}{r}
278 \\
\times \quad 19 \\
\hline
2502 \\
2780 \\
\hline
5282
\end{array}
$$

2502 ⟵ 278 × 9
2780 ⟵ 278 × 10

7. Multiply.
    (a) 20×60 (b) 50×80 (c) 70×90
    (d) 500×30 (e) 40×600 (f) 400×50

8. Estimate the value of 32×68.

32×68
↓   ↓
30×70

$30 \times 70 = $

The value of 32×68 is about .

9. Estimate the value of 48×315.

48×315
↓   ↓
50×300

$50 \times 300 = $

The value of 48×315 is about .

10. Estimate and then multiply.
    (a) 49×18 (b) 21×72 (c) 62×47
    (d) 412×23 (e) 383×58 (f) 685×32
    (g) 51×490 (h) 69×786 (i) 88×594

Workbook Exercises 15 & 16

PRACTICE 2B

Estimate and then find the value of each of the following:

	(a)	(b)	(c)
1.	2907 × 4	6032 × 5	7902 × 7
2.	4170 ÷ 6	5616 ÷ 8	8019 ÷ 9
3.	48 × 11	61 × 29	88 × 67
4.	101 × 13	289 × 53	786 × 78

5. Miguel delivers 165 copies of a newspaper every day.
   How many copies of the newspaper will he deliver in 30 days?

6. Tom bought 15 sheets of stamps.
   If there were 25 stamps on each sheet, how many stamps did he buy?

7. After buying 12 chairs at $128 each, Catherine had $342 left.
   How much money did she have at first?

8. 300 children are divided into two groups.
   There are 50 more children in the first group than in the second group.
   How many children are there in the second group?

9. The difference between two numbers is 2184.
   If the bigger number is 3 times the smaller number, find the sum of the two numbers.

10. Mrs. Garcia saved $2001 in two years.
    She saved $65 a month in the first 15 months.
    She saved the same amount every month in the next 9 months.
    How much did she save a month in the next 9 months?

40

REVIEW A

1. What is the value of the digit **6** in each of the following?
   (a) 39,1**6**4   (b) **6**,083   (c) **6**2,375

2. Write the following in figures.
   (a) Twenty-four thousand, thirty-eight
   (b) Seventy-four thousand, two

3. Write the following in words.
   (a) 42,310   (b) 15,206   (c) 20,815

4. Bill has $2486 in his savings account.
   Round off this amount of money to the nearest $100.

5. (a) Write down a common factor of 12 and 20.
   (b) Write down a common multiple of 8 and 12.

6. Find the product of
   (a) 64 and 25   (b) 1250 and 8

7. Find the quotient and remainder when
   (a) 1026 is divided by 3   (b) 5000 is divided by 6
   (c) 4984 is divided by 7   (d) 2831 is divided by 9

8. A shopkeeper packed 3284 pieces of soap into 6 equal packages.
   How many pieces of soap were there in each package?
   How many pieces of soap were left over?

9. Mary had 1240 picture cards.
   She kept 80 cards for herself and gave the rest to a group of children.
   Each child received 8 cards.
   How many children were there in the group?

10. 3000 exercise books are arranged into 3 piles.
    The first pile has 10 more books than the second pile.
    The number of books in the second pile is twice the number of books in the third pile.
    How many books are there in the third pile?

Fractions

1 Adding Fractions

Lila drank $\frac{1}{5}$ liter of milk.

Her brother drank $\frac{2}{5}$ liter of milk.

How much milk did they drink altogether?

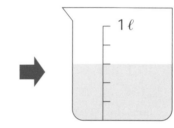

$$\frac{1}{5} + \frac{2}{5} = \blacksquare$$

1 fifth + 2 fifths
= 3 fifths

They drank $\blacksquare$ liter of milk altogether.

1. Find the sum of $\frac{2}{5}$ and $\frac{3}{5}$.

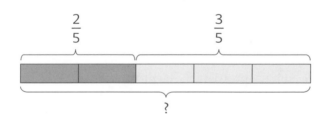

2 fifths + 3 fifths
= 1 whole

$$\frac{2}{5} + \frac{3}{5} = \blacksquare$$

42

2. (a) Add $\frac{3}{8}$ and $\frac{2}{8}$.

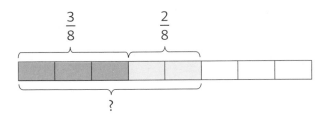

$$\frac{3}{8} + \frac{2}{8} = \frac{\blacksquare}{8}$$

(b) Add $\frac{5}{8}$ and $\frac{1}{8}$.

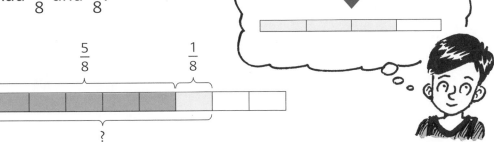

$$\frac{5}{8} + \frac{1}{8} = \frac{\blacksquare}{8}$$
$$= \blacksquare$$

3. Add.

(a) $\frac{1}{9} + \frac{4}{9}$ (b) $\frac{2}{7} + \frac{2}{7}$ (c) $\frac{4}{6} + \frac{1}{6}$

(d) $\frac{1}{6} + \frac{3}{6}$ (e) $\frac{1}{4} + \frac{3}{4}$ (f) $\frac{3}{10} + \frac{5}{10}$

(g) $\frac{3}{7} + \frac{4}{7}$ (h) $\frac{2}{9} + \frac{4}{9}$ (i) $\frac{5}{12} + \frac{1}{12}$

(j) $\frac{2}{5} + \frac{2}{5} + \frac{1}{5}$ (k) $\frac{3}{7} + \frac{3}{7} + \frac{1}{7}$ (l) $\frac{2}{9} + \frac{2}{9} + \frac{2}{9}$

Workbook Exercise 17

4. Add $\frac{1}{2}$ and $\frac{1}{4}$.

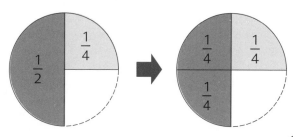

1 half = 2 quarters

$\frac{1}{2} + \frac{1}{4} = \blacksquare$

5. Add $\frac{2}{3}$ and $\frac{1}{6}$.

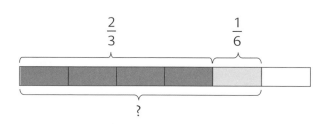

$\frac{2}{3} = \frac{\blacksquare}{6}$

$\frac{2}{3} + \frac{1}{6} = \frac{\blacksquare}{6} + \frac{1}{6}$

$= \frac{\blacksquare}{6}$

6. What are the missing numbers?

(a) $\frac{3}{8} + \frac{1}{4}$

$= \frac{3}{8} + \frac{\blacksquare}{8}$

$= \frac{\blacksquare}{8}$

(b) $\frac{2}{3} + \frac{1}{9}$

$= \frac{\blacksquare}{9} + \frac{1}{9}$

$= \frac{\blacksquare}{9}$

44

7. Add $\frac{1}{5}$ and $\frac{3}{10}$.

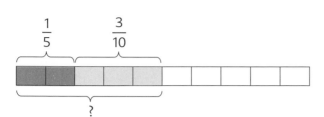

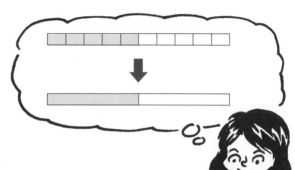

$\frac{1}{5} + \frac{3}{10} = \frac{\blacksquare}{10} + \frac{3}{10}$

$= \frac{\blacksquare}{10}$

$= \blacksquare$

8. What are the missing numbers?

(a) $\frac{1}{3} + \frac{1}{6}$

$= \frac{\blacksquare}{6} + \frac{1}{6}$

$= \frac{\blacksquare}{6}$

$= \blacksquare$

(b) $\frac{1}{2} + \frac{3}{10}$

$= \frac{\blacksquare}{10} + \frac{3}{10}$

$= \frac{\blacksquare}{10}$

$= \blacksquare$

9. Add.

(a) $\frac{1}{2} + \frac{1}{8}$

(b) $\frac{1}{4} + \frac{2}{12}$

(c) $\frac{2}{3} + \frac{1}{9}$

(d) $\frac{1}{2} + \frac{1}{6}$

(e) $\frac{2}{5} + \frac{1}{10}$

(f) $\frac{2}{3} + \frac{1}{12}$

(g) $\frac{1}{5} + \frac{3}{10}$

(h) $\frac{1}{6} + \frac{7}{12}$

(i) $\frac{3}{4} + \frac{1}{12}$

(j) $\frac{1}{3} + \frac{1}{9} + \frac{1}{9}$

(k) $\frac{1}{2} + \frac{1}{4} + \frac{1}{4}$

(l) $\frac{1}{4} + \frac{1}{8} + \frac{3}{8}$

Workbook Exercise 18

2 Subtracting Fractions

Devi had $\frac{7}{8}$ of a pie.

She ate $\frac{2}{8}$ of the pie.
What fraction of the pie was left?

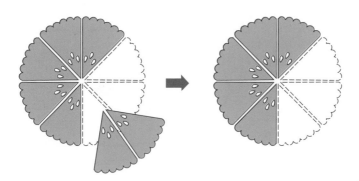

$$\frac{7}{8} - \frac{2}{8} = \blacksquare$$

7 eighths — 2 eighths = 5 eighths

$\blacksquare$ of the pie was left.

1. Find the difference between $\frac{4}{5}$ and $\frac{3}{5}$.

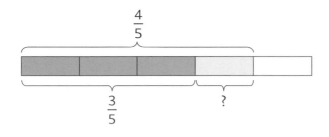

$$\frac{4}{5} - \frac{3}{5} = \blacksquare$$

4 fifths — 3 fifths = 1 fifth

2. Subtract $\frac{3}{10}$ from 1.

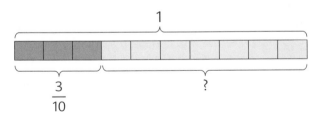

$$1 = \frac{10}{10}$$

$\frac{3}{10}$?

$$1 - \frac{3}{10} = \blacksquare$$

3. Subtract $\frac{1}{8}$ from $\frac{5}{8}$.

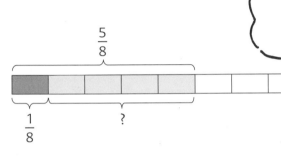

$\frac{5}{8}$

$\frac{1}{8}$?

$$\frac{5}{8} - \frac{1}{8} = \frac{\blacksquare}{8}$$
$$= \blacksquare$$

4. Subtract.

(a) $\frac{4}{5} - \frac{1}{5}$

(b) $\frac{6}{8} - \frac{5}{8}$

(c) $\frac{7}{9} - \frac{3}{9}$

(d) $\frac{3}{4} - \frac{1}{4}$

(e) $\frac{7}{10} - \frac{3}{10}$

(f) $\frac{8}{12} - \frac{5}{12}$

(g) $1 - \frac{2}{9}$

(h) $1 - \frac{9}{10}$

(i) $1 - \frac{7}{12}$

(j) $1 - \frac{2}{5} - \frac{2}{5}$

(k) $\frac{7}{8} - \frac{1}{8} - \frac{3}{8}$

(l) $\frac{8}{9} - \frac{1}{9} - \frac{4}{9}$

Workbook Exercise 19

5. Subtract $\frac{1}{8}$ from $\frac{1}{2}$.

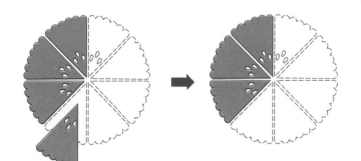

1 half = 4 eighths

$$\frac{1}{2} - \frac{1}{8} = \blacksquare$$

6. Subtract $\frac{1}{2}$ from $\frac{7}{8}$.

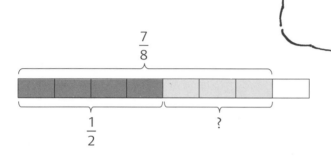

$$\frac{1}{2} = \frac{\blacksquare}{8}$$

$$\frac{7}{8} - \frac{1}{2} = \frac{7}{8} - \frac{\blacksquare}{8}$$

$$= \frac{\blacksquare}{8}$$

7. What are the missing numbers?

(a) $\frac{3}{4} - \frac{1}{8}$

$$= \frac{\blacksquare}{8} - \frac{1}{8}$$

$$= \frac{\blacksquare}{8}$$

(b) $\frac{7}{10} - \frac{2}{5}$

$$= \frac{7}{10} - \frac{\blacksquare}{10}$$

$$= \frac{\blacksquare}{10}$$

8. Subtract $\frac{5}{12}$ from $\frac{3}{4}$.

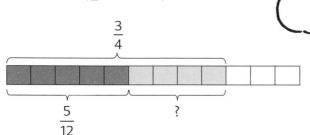

$\frac{3}{4} = \frac{\blacksquare}{12}$

$\frac{3}{4} - \frac{5}{12} = \frac{\blacksquare}{12} - \frac{5}{12}$

$= \frac{\blacksquare}{12}$

$= \blacksquare$

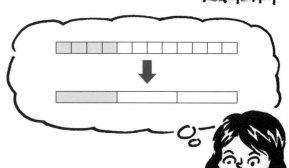

9. What are the missing numbers?

(a) $\frac{7}{10} - \frac{1}{2}$

$= \frac{7}{10} - \frac{\blacksquare}{10}$

$= \frac{\blacksquare}{10}$

$= \blacksquare$

(b) $\frac{2}{3} - \frac{5}{12}$

$= \frac{\blacksquare}{12} - \frac{5}{12}$

$= \frac{\blacksquare}{12}$

$= \blacksquare$

10. Subtract.

(a) $\frac{5}{9} - \frac{1}{3}$

(b) $\frac{3}{4} - \frac{3}{8}$

(c) $\frac{4}{5} - \frac{7}{10}$

(d) $\frac{5}{6} - \frac{1}{2}$

(e) $\frac{1}{3} - \frac{1}{12}$

(f) $\frac{7}{10} - \frac{1}{5}$

(g) $\frac{1}{2} - \frac{1}{10}$

(h) $\frac{3}{4} - \frac{5}{12}$

(i) $\frac{5}{6} - \frac{7}{12}$

(j) $1 - \frac{1}{2} - \frac{1}{4}$

(k) $1 - \frac{1}{2} - \frac{1}{6}$

(l) $\frac{2}{3} - \frac{1}{6} - \frac{1}{3}$

Workbook Exercises 20 & 21

PRACTICE 3A

Add or subtract.

	(a)	(b)	(c)
1.	$\dfrac{1}{5} + \dfrac{3}{5}$	$\dfrac{2}{6} + \dfrac{3}{6}$	$\dfrac{3}{10} + \dfrac{4}{10}$
2.	$\dfrac{8}{10} - \dfrac{5}{10}$	$\dfrac{5}{7} - \dfrac{2}{7}$	$1 - \dfrac{2}{9}$
3.	$\dfrac{3}{8} + \dfrac{4}{8}$	$\dfrac{2}{3} + \dfrac{1}{3}$	$\dfrac{2}{9} + \dfrac{5}{9}$
4.	$1 - \dfrac{3}{5}$	$\dfrac{5}{6} - \dfrac{1}{6}$	$\dfrac{3}{4} - \dfrac{1}{4}$
5.	$\dfrac{3}{10} + \dfrac{3}{10}$	$\dfrac{1}{12} + \dfrac{5}{12}$	$\dfrac{3}{11} + \dfrac{5}{11}$

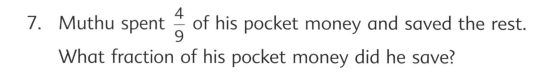

6. Sally ate $\dfrac{1}{8}$ of a cake and her sister ate $\dfrac{3}{8}$ of it.
   What fraction of the cake did they eat altogether?

7. Muthu spent $\dfrac{4}{9}$ of his pocket money and saved the rest.
   What fraction of his pocket money did he save?

8. Minghua spent $\dfrac{3}{7}$ of his money on a book and the rest on a racket.
   What fraction of his money was spent on the racket?

9. Fatimah baked a pie.

   She ate $\dfrac{1}{6}$ of the pie and gave $\dfrac{3}{6}$ of the pie to her friends.
   What fraction of the pie did she have left?

PRACTICE 3B

Add or subtract.

	(a)	(b)	(c)
1.	$\dfrac{7}{8} - \dfrac{3}{4}$	$\dfrac{2}{3} - \dfrac{1}{12}$	$1 - \dfrac{3}{10}$
2.	$\dfrac{2}{9} + \dfrac{1}{3}$	$\dfrac{1}{6} + \dfrac{2}{3}$	$\dfrac{5}{12} + \dfrac{1}{4}$
3.	$\dfrac{1}{6} - \dfrac{1}{12}$	$\dfrac{3}{8} - \dfrac{1}{4}$	$\dfrac{4}{5} - \dfrac{3}{10}$
4.	$\dfrac{1}{2} + \dfrac{3}{8}$	$\dfrac{1}{3} + \dfrac{1}{12}$	$\dfrac{2}{8} + \dfrac{3}{4}$
5.	$\dfrac{1}{4} + \dfrac{3}{8} + \dfrac{1}{4}$	$\dfrac{7}{8} - \dfrac{1}{8} - \dfrac{3}{8}$	$1 - \dfrac{1}{5} - \dfrac{3}{10}$

6. Mary has $\dfrac{3}{4}$ litre of orange juice.

   She drinks $\dfrac{1}{2}$ litre of it.

   How much orange juice does she have left?

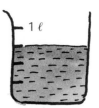

7. Mr. Johnson bought a can of paint.

   He used $\dfrac{1}{2}$ of it to paint a table.

   He used $\dfrac{1}{8}$ of it to paint a book shelf.

   How much paint did he use altogether?

8. Meredith bought $\dfrac{2}{5}$ kg of shrimps.

   Courtney bought $\dfrac{1}{10}$ kg of shrimps less than Meredith.

   (a) Find the weight of the shrimps bought by Courtney.
   (b) Find the total weight of the shrimps bought by them.

51

3 Mixed Numbers

This strip of paper is longer than 1 m.

1 m $\frac{1}{2}$ m

It is $1\frac{1}{2}$ m long.

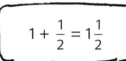

$$1 + \frac{1}{2} = 1\frac{1}{2}$$

There are $2\frac{1}{2}$ watermelons.

$$2 + \frac{1}{2} = 2\frac{1}{2}$$

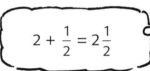

The total amount of water is $3\frac{3}{4}$ liters.

$$3 + \frac{3}{4} = 3\frac{3}{4}$$

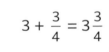

$1\frac{1}{2}$, $2\frac{1}{2}$ and $3\frac{3}{4}$ are **mixed numbers**.

When we add a whole number and a fraction, the result is a mixed number.

1. Write a mixed number for each of the following:

(a)

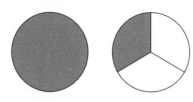

1 whole 1 third = ■

$$1 + \frac{1}{3} = ■$$

(b)

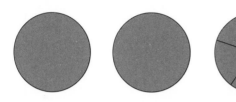

2 wholes 3 fifths = ■

(c)

2 wholes 1 sixth = ■

2. What number does each letter represent?

(a)

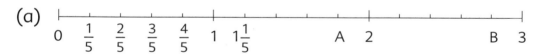

$0 \quad \frac{1}{5} \quad \frac{2}{5} \quad \frac{3}{5} \quad \frac{4}{5} \quad 1 \quad 1\frac{1}{5} \qquad A \quad 2 \qquad\qquad B \quad 3$

(b)

$0 \quad \frac{1}{8} \quad \frac{2}{8} \quad \frac{3}{8} \quad \frac{4}{8} \quad \frac{5}{8} \quad \frac{6}{8} \quad \frac{7}{8} \quad 1 \quad 1\frac{1}{8} \qquad C \qquad\qquad D \quad 2$

3. Find the value of

(a) $3 + \frac{2}{3}$

(b) $\frac{4}{5} + 2$

(c) $\frac{7}{10} + 4$

(d) $2 - \frac{1}{4}$

(e) $3 - \frac{1}{5}$

(f) $5 - \frac{2}{3}$

Workbook Exercise 22

④ Improper Fractions

What is the length of each of the following strips of paper?

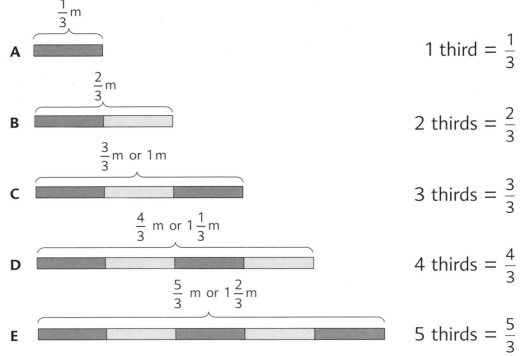

A $\frac{1}{3}$ m   1 third $= \frac{1}{3}$

B $\frac{2}{3}$ m   2 thirds $= \frac{2}{3}$

C $\frac{3}{3}$ m or 1 m   3 thirds $= \frac{3}{3}$

D $\frac{4}{3}$ m or $1\frac{1}{3}$ m   4 thirds $= \frac{4}{3}$

E $\frac{5}{3}$ m or $1\frac{2}{3}$ m   5 thirds $= \frac{5}{3}$

$\frac{3}{3}$, $\frac{4}{3}$ and $\frac{5}{3}$ are **improper fractions**.

An improper fraction is equal to or greater than 1.

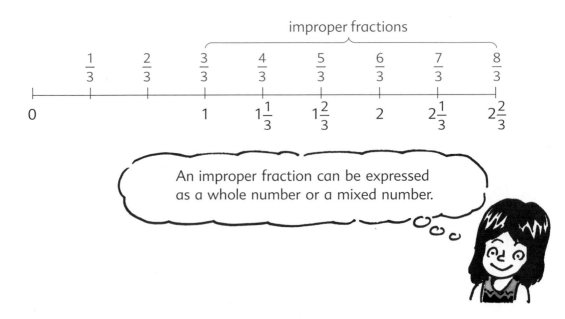

An improper fraction can be expressed as a whole number or a mixed number.

1. How many halves are there in $3\frac{1}{2}$?

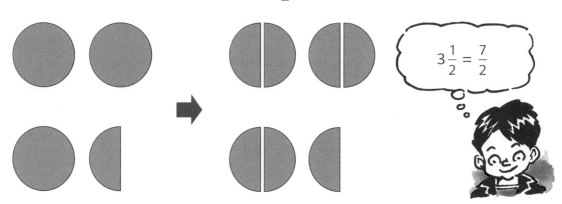

$$3\frac{1}{2} = \frac{7}{2}$$

There are ■ halves in $3\frac{1}{2}$.

2. Write an improper fraction for each of the following:

(a)

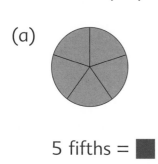

$$\frac{1}{5} + \frac{1}{5} + \frac{1}{5} + \frac{1}{5} + \frac{1}{5} = ■$$

5 fifths = ■

(b)

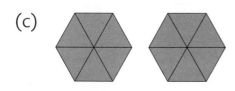

7 quarters = ■

(c)

12 sixths = ■

Workbook Exercise 23

3. Change the improper fractions to mixed numbers.

(a) $\dfrac{7}{5} = \dfrac{5}{5} + \dfrac{2}{5}$

$= 1 + \dfrac{2}{5}$

$= 1\dfrac{\blacksquare}{5}$

(b) $\dfrac{14}{5} = \dfrac{10}{5} + \dfrac{4}{5}$

$= 2 + \dfrac{4}{5}$

$= \blacksquare$

4. Change $\dfrac{13}{6}$ to a mixed number.

$\dfrac{13}{6} = \dfrac{12}{6} + \dfrac{1}{6}$

$= 2 + \dfrac{1}{6}$

$= \blacksquare$

$\dfrac{6}{6} = 1$

$\dfrac{12}{6} = 2$

5. Express each of the following as a mixed number or a whole number.

(a) $\dfrac{17}{4}$ (b) $\dfrac{10}{3}$ (c) $\dfrac{8}{2}$ (d) $\dfrac{12}{5}$

Workbook Exercise 24

6. Change the mixed numbers to improper fractions.

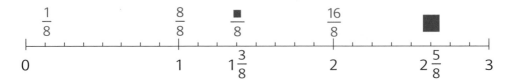

(a) $1\dfrac{3}{8} = 1 + \dfrac{3}{8}$

$= \dfrac{8}{8} + \dfrac{3}{8}$

$= \dfrac{\blacksquare}{8}$

(b) $2\dfrac{5}{8} = 2 + \dfrac{5}{8}$

$= \dfrac{16}{8} + \dfrac{5}{8}$

$= \blacksquare$

7. Change $3\frac{1}{6}$ to an improper fraction.

$$3\frac{1}{6} = 3 + \frac{1}{6}$$

$$= \frac{18}{6} + \frac{1}{6}$$

$$= \blacksquare$$

$$1 = \frac{6}{6}$$

$$3 = \frac{18}{6}$$

8. Express each of the following as an improper fraction.

(a) $1\frac{4}{5}$ (b) $2\frac{2}{3}$ (c) $2\frac{1}{4}$ (d) $2\frac{5}{6}$

9. Find the missing numerator in each of the following:

(a) $2\frac{1}{3} = 1\frac{\blacksquare}{3}$ (b) $2\frac{2}{5} = 1\frac{\blacksquare}{5}$ (c) $3\frac{1}{4} = 2\frac{\blacksquare}{4}$

(d) $3\frac{1}{2} = 2\frac{\blacksquare}{2}$ (e) $4\frac{1}{6} = 3\frac{\blacksquare}{6}$ (f) $4\frac{3}{4} = 3\frac{\blacksquare}{4}$

Workbook Exercise 25

10. Express each of the following as a whole number or a mixed number in its simplest form.

(a) $\frac{10}{4}$ (b) $\frac{12}{3}$ (c) $2\frac{5}{10}$ (d) $2\frac{8}{12}$

(e) $2\frac{8}{5}$ (f) $3\frac{7}{4}$ (g) $1\frac{6}{8}$ (h) $2\frac{6}{3}$

11. Add. Give each answer in its simplest form.

(a) $\frac{5}{6} + \frac{5}{6}$ (b) $\frac{3}{5} + \frac{4}{5}$ (c) $\frac{3}{4} + \frac{1}{4}$

(d) $\frac{6}{7} + \frac{5}{7}$ (e) $\frac{7}{10} + \frac{4}{5}$ (f) $\frac{7}{8} + \frac{3}{4}$

12. Subtract. Give each answer in its simplest form.

(a) $3 - \frac{3}{4}$ (b) $2 - \frac{3}{8}$ (c) $4 - \frac{1}{2}$

(d) $2 - \frac{3}{10}$ (e) $2 - \frac{4}{5}$ (f) $3 - \frac{5}{7}$

Workbook Exercise 26

57

⑤ Fraction of a Set

2 out of 5 children are girls.
What fraction of the children are girls?

2 out of 5 groups of children are girls.
What fraction of the children are girls?

2 out of 5 is $\frac{2}{5}$.

1. What fraction of each set is shaded?

(a)

(b)

(c)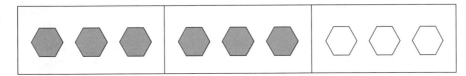

(d)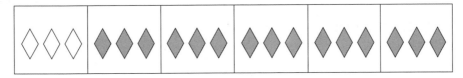

Workbook Exercise 27

2. What is $\frac{1}{3}$ of 12?

$\frac{1}{3}$ of 12 = ■

Divide 12 into 3 equal groups.

One group is $\frac{1}{3}$ of 12.

$\frac{1}{3}$ of 12 is 4.

3. Find the value of $\frac{3}{4}$ of 20.

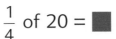

$\frac{1}{4}$ of 20 = ■

$\frac{3}{4}$ of 20 = ■

Workbook Exercise 28

59

$$\frac{1}{4} \times 20 = \frac{1 \times 20}{4}$$

$$= \blacksquare$$

$\frac{1}{4}$ of 20 is the same as $\frac{1}{4} \times 20$.

$$\frac{3}{4} \times 20 = \frac{3 \times 20}{4}$$

$$= \blacksquare$$

$\frac{3}{4}$ of 20 is the same as $\frac{3}{4} \times 20$.

4. Find the value of $\frac{5}{6}$ of 18.

$$\frac{5}{6} \times 18 = \frac{5 \times 18}{6}$$

$$= \blacksquare$$

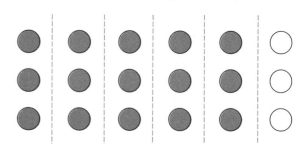

Workbook Exercise 29

5. Find the value of $\frac{3}{4}$ of 9.

$$\frac{3}{4} \times 9 = \frac{3 \times 9}{4}$$

$$= \blacksquare$$

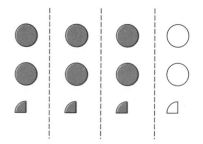

6. Find the value of

(a) $\frac{1}{2}$ of 12

(b) $\frac{1}{5}$ of 20

(c) $\frac{1}{6}$ of 4

(d) $\frac{2}{3}$ of 9

(e) $\frac{3}{8}$ of 16

(f) $\frac{2}{3}$ of 10

Workbook Exercise 30

7. Kelley buys 24 flowers.

$\frac{2}{3}$ of them are white.

How many white flowers are there?

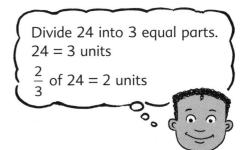

Divide 24 into 3 equal parts.
24 = 3 units
$\frac{2}{3}$ of 24 = 2 units

Method 1:

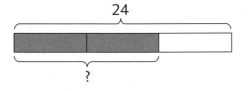

24

?

3 units = 24

1 unit = ■

2 units = ■

There are ■ white flowers.

Method 2:

$\frac{2}{3} \times 24 = $ ■

There are ■ white flowers.

$\frac{2}{3}$ of 24 is the same as

$\frac{2}{3} \times 24$.

Workbook Exercise 31

8. There are 8 coins.
6 of them are ten-cent coins.
What fraction of the coins are ten-cent coins?

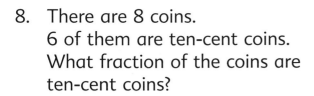

6 out of 8 is $\frac{6}{8}$.

$\frac{\cancel{6}^{3}}{\cancel{8}_{4}} = \frac{3}{4}$

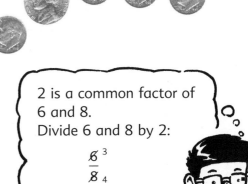

2 is a common factor of
6 and 8.
Divide 6 and 8 by 2:

$\frac{\cancel{6}^{3}}{\cancel{8}_{4}}$

■ of the coins are ten-cent coins.

9. Minghua had 42 stamps.
   He lost 6 of them.
   What fraction of the stamps did he lose?

   $$\frac{6}{42} = \blacksquare$$

   6 out of 42 is $\frac{6}{42}$.

   Express $\frac{6}{42}$ in its simplest form.

   He lost $\blacksquare$ of the stamps.

10. Jenny's handspan is 16 cm.
    What fraction of 1 m is 16 cm?

    $$\frac{16}{100} = \blacksquare$$

    ←— 16 cm —→

    1 m = 100 cm

    16 cm is $\blacksquare$ of 1 m.

Workbook Exercise 32

11. David spent $\frac{2}{5}$ of his money on a storybook.

    The storybook cost $20.
    How much money did he have at first?

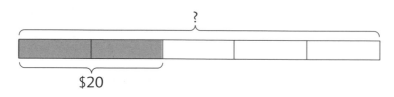

$20

    2 units = $20
    1 unit = $$\blacksquare$
    5 units = $$\blacksquare$
He had $$\blacksquare$ at first.

Workbook Exercise 33

12. Meiling had $20.

She used $\frac{2}{5}$ of it to buy a book.

How much did she have left?

Method 1:

$$\frac{2}{5} \times 20 = \frac{2 \times \cancel{20}^{4}}{\cancel{5}_{1}}$$
$$= 8$$

First, I find the amount of money she used.

She used $8.

$$20 - 8 = \blacksquare$$

She had $\blacksquare$ left.

Method 2:

$$1 - \frac{2}{5} = \frac{3}{5}$$

First, I find what fraction of the money is left.

She had $\frac{3}{5}$ of her money left.

$$\frac{3}{5} \times 20 = \blacksquare$$

She had $\blacksquare$ left.

Method 3:

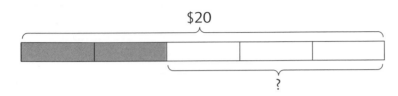

$20

?

5 units = $20
1 unit = $\blacksquare$
3 units = $\blacksquare$
She had $\blacksquare$ left.

13. 48 children went to the zoo.

$\frac{3}{8}$ of them were girls.

How many boys were there?

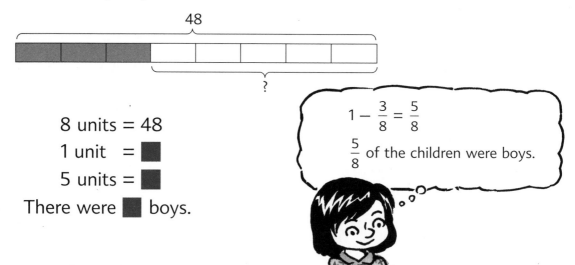

8 units = 48

1 unit = ■

5 units = ■

There were ■ boys.

$1 - \frac{3}{8} = \frac{5}{8}$

$\frac{5}{8}$ of the children were boys.

14. In a class of 40 students, 25 are boys.
Express the number of girls as a fraction of the class.

Method 1:

$40 - 25 = 15$

There are 15 girls.

$\frac{15}{40} = $ ■

■ of the class are girls.

First, I find the number of girls.

Method 2:

$\frac{25}{40} = \frac{5}{8}$

$\frac{5}{8}$ of the class are boys.

$1 - \frac{5}{8} = $ ■

■ of the class are girls.

First, I express the number of boys as a fraction of the class.

Workbook Exercises 34 & 35

PRACTICE 3C

Multiply. Give each answer in its simplest form.

	(a)	(b)	(c)	(d)
1.	$\frac{1}{3} \times 18$	$\frac{3}{4} \times 32$	$\frac{1}{6} \times 4$	$\frac{5}{9} \times 15$
2.	$36 \times \frac{1}{4}$	$15 \times \frac{2}{5}$	$6 \times \frac{1}{8}$	$10 \times \frac{3}{4}$

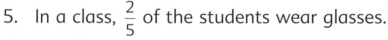

3. Peter had a board 3 m long.

   He used $\frac{3}{4}$ of its length as a bookshelf.

   How long was the bookshelf?

4. Jane practices on the piano for $\frac{3}{4}$ hour a day.

   How many hours does she practice on the piano in 5 days?

5. In a class, $\frac{2}{5}$ of the students wear glasses.

   (a) What fraction of the students do **not** wear glasses?
   (b) If 16 students wear glasses, how many students are there altogether?

6. Aminah bought 30 eggs.

   She used $\frac{2}{3}$ of the eggs to bake cakes.

   How many eggs did she have left?

7. Lily bought some picture cards.

   She gave $\frac{1}{3}$ of them to Matthew.

   If she gave 8 picture cards to Matthew, how many picture cards did she buy?

8. Kevin spent $\frac{1}{4}$ of his money on a storybook.

   If the storybook cost $6, how much money did he have at first?

REVIEW B

1. Write the following in figures.
   (a) Seven thousand, three
   (b) Fifteen thousand, two hundred twelve

2. Write the following in words.
   (a) 4660   (b) 35,600   (c) 47,019   (d) 52,473

3. Arrange the numbers in increasing order.
   (a) 74,355, 75,435, 47,355, 74,535
   (b) 32,223, 33,222, 23,322, 23,232

4. (a) What number is 100 more than 15,960?
   (b) What number is 1000 less than 70,516?

5. In **27,965**, the digit **2** stands for 2 × ■.
   What is the missing number in the ■?

6. Round off each number to the nearest ten.
   (a) 413   (b) 685   (c) 5968

7. Round off each number to the nearest hundred.
   (a) 683   (b) 5608   (c) 7449

8. (a) Find the product of 15 and 306.
   (b) Find the quotient and remainder when 3650 is divided by 8.

9. Find the missing factor in each of the following:
   (a) 45 = 5 × ■   (b) 16 = 2 × ■
   (c) 27 = ■ × 9   (d) 18 = ■ × 9

10. (a) Find a common factor of 9 and 30.
    (b) Find a common multiple of 6 and 9.

11. Add or subtract. Give each answer in its simplest form.

(a) $\dfrac{1}{3} + \dfrac{5}{12}$

(b) $\dfrac{4}{9} + \dfrac{1}{3}$

(c) $\dfrac{1}{12} + \dfrac{5}{6}$

(d) $\dfrac{1}{2} - \dfrac{3}{10}$

(e) $\dfrac{2}{3} - \dfrac{5}{12}$

(f) $\dfrac{7}{8} - \dfrac{3}{4}$

12. What fraction of each figure is shaded?
Give each answer in its simplest form.

(a)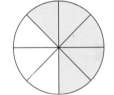

(b)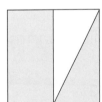

(c)

(d)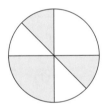

(e)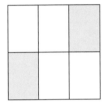

(f)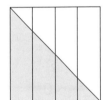

13. What fraction of each set is shaded?
Give each answer in its simplest form.

(a)

(b)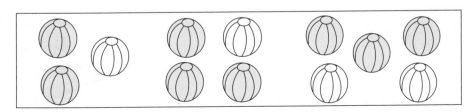

14. Arrange the numbers in increasing order.

$\frac{1}{3}$ $\frac{3}{5}$ $\frac{1}{12}$ $\frac{4}{4}$ $\frac{3}{2}$

15. Find the missing numerator or denominator.

(a) $\frac{3}{5} = \frac{\blacksquare}{10}$

(b) $\frac{1}{6} = \frac{3}{\blacksquare}$

(c) $\frac{6}{9} = \frac{\blacksquare}{3}$

(d) $\frac{8}{12} = \frac{2}{\blacksquare}$

16. Express each of the following fractions in its simplest form.

(a) $\frac{8}{10}$

(b) $\frac{2}{12}$

(c) $1\frac{2}{6}$

(d) $2\frac{3}{12}$

17. Express each of the following as a whole number or a mixed number in its simplest form.

(a) $\frac{10}{3}$

(b) $\frac{15}{5}$

(c) $\frac{18}{4}$

(d) $\frac{23}{7}$

18. Express each of the following as an improper fraction.

(a) $1\frac{4}{7}$

(b) $2\frac{4}{5}$

(c) $3\frac{1}{8}$

(d) $2\frac{9}{10}$

19. 10 girls had pizza for lunch.

Each girl ate $\frac{1}{4}$ of a pizza.

How many pizzas did they eat altogether?

20. Loraine bought a bottle of cooking oil.

    She used $\frac{3}{10}$ of the cooking oil.

    If she used 150 g of cooking oil, how much cooking oil did she buy?

21. Jordan poured 20 liters of water into an empty fish tank.

    If $\frac{5}{6}$ of the fish tank was filled, find the capacity of the tank.

22. Jennifer made 100 sandwiches for a children's party.

    The children ate $\frac{3}{4}$ of the sandwiches.

    How many sandwiches were left?

23.

$18 $24 $36

Lily bought these items at half of the given prices.
How much did she spend altogether?

24. $\frac{4}{5}$ of the children in a choir are girls.
    (a) What fraction of the children are boys?
    (b) If there are 8 boys, how many children are there altogether?
    (c) How many more girls than boys are there?

Tables and Graphs

1 Presenting Data

These cards show the names and weights of five children.

Name : Rachel
Weight : 38 kg

Name : Veronica
Weight : 39 kg

Name : Tasha
Weight : 38 kg

Name : Roy
Weight : 43 kg

Name : Juan
Weight : 40 kg

The data can be presented in the form of a table like this:

Name	Weight
Rachel	38 kg
Veronica	39 kg
Tasha	38 kg
Roy	43 kg
Juan	40 kg

The data can also be presented in a bar graph:

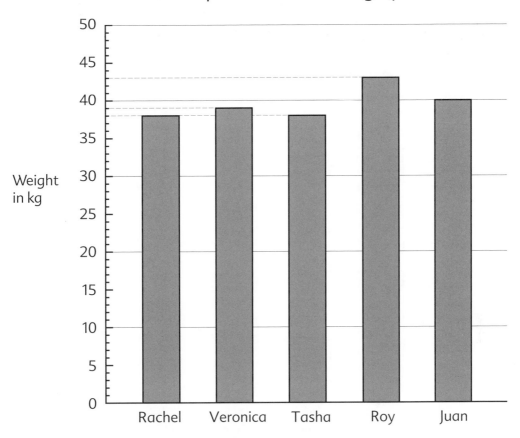

1. This table shows the number of storybooks read by four children in one month.

Name	Number of books
David	8
Pablo	16
Lauren	14
Rosa	10

(a) Who read the greatest number of storybooks in one month?

(b) How many more storybooks did Lauren read than David in one month?

(c) Draw a bar graph to show the data given in the table.

2. The bar graph shows the number of cars sold by Patrick in 6 months.
   Use the graph to answer the questions which follow.

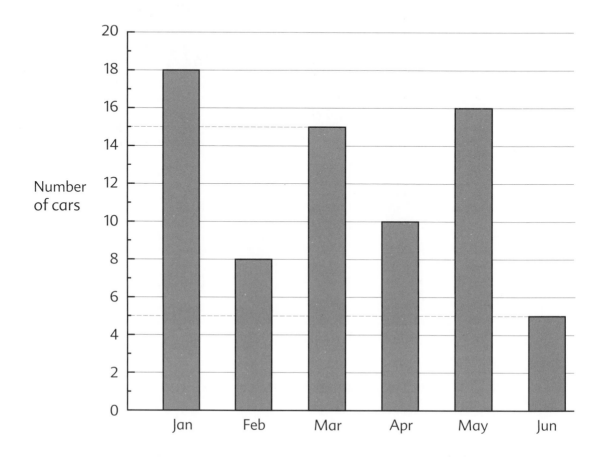

(a) How many cars did Patrick sell in March?

(b) In which months did Patrick sell less than 10 cars?

(c) In which month did Patrick sell the greatest number of cars?

(d) How many more cars were sold in May than in April?

(e) In which month were half as many cars sold as in May?

3. Make a table to show the data given in the bar graph above.

Workbook Exercises 36 to 38

4. The table shows the number of people who attended four courses in a community center.
Use the table to answer the questions which follow.

Course	Men	Women
Cooking	6	21
Art	14	11
Computer	25	24
Dancing	12	18

(a) How many people attended the cooking course?

(b) How many more women than men attended the dancing course?

(c) How many more people attended the computer course than the art course?

5. In a class of 22 boys and 20 girls, 8 boys wear glasses and 15 girls **do not** wear glasses.

(a) Copy and complete the following table.

	Number of boys	Number of girls	Total number
Wearing glasses	8		
Not wearing glasses		15	
Total number =	22	20	42

(b) How many students wear glasses?

(c) How many students **do not** wear glasses?

Workbook Exercises 39 & 40

Angles

1 Measuring Angles

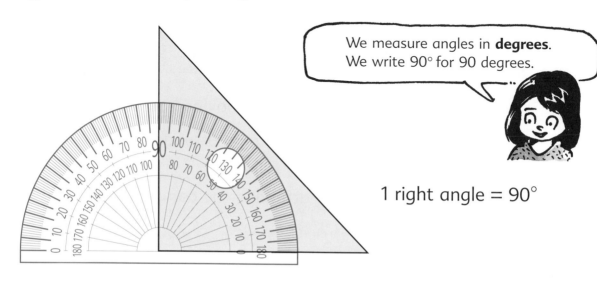

We measure angles in **degrees**.
We write 90° for 90 degrees.

1 right angle = 90°

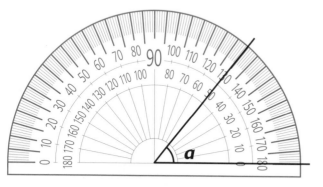

Angle *a* is smaller than
a right angle.
It is 50 degrees.

We write:
$\angle a = 50°$

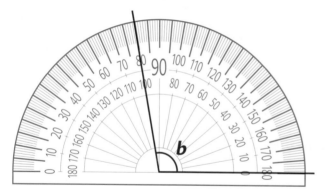

Angle *b* is greater than
a right angle.
It is 100 degrees.

We write:
$\angle b = 100°$

1. What is the size of each angle?

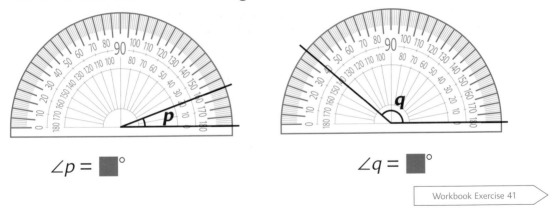

∠p = ▇°   ∠q = ▇°

Workbook Exercise 41

2. Estimate and then measure each of the following angles.

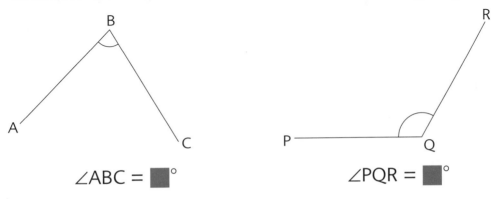

∠ABC = ▇°   ∠PQR = ▇°

3. (a) Draw an angle equal to 35°.

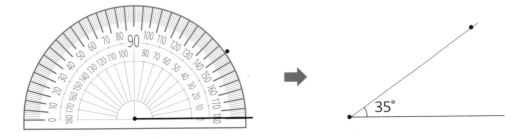

35°

(b) Draw an angle equal to 165°.

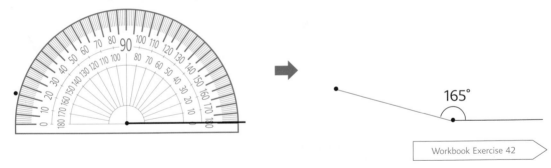

165°

Workbook Exercise 42

4.

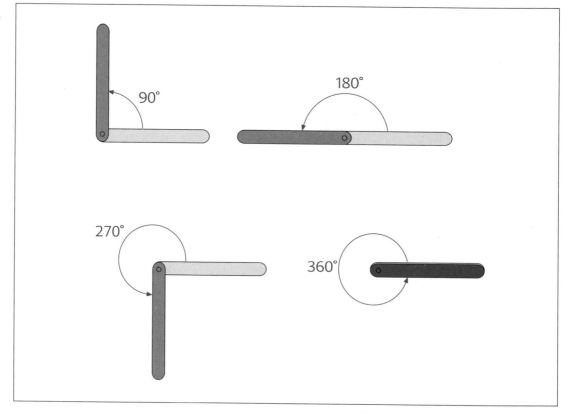

A $\frac{1}{4}$ - turn is 1 right angle. It is 90°.

A $\frac{1}{2}$ - turn is 2 right angles. It is ■°.

A $\frac{3}{4}$ - turn is 3 right angles. It is ■°.

A complete turn is 4 right angles. It is ■°.

5. $\angle x$ is between 180° and 360°.

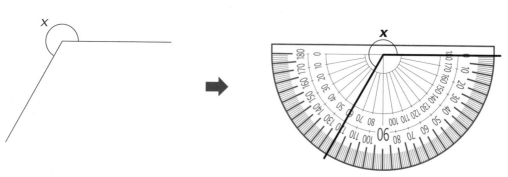

$\angle x = 360° - 120° = $ ■°

6. ∠p is between 180° and 360°.

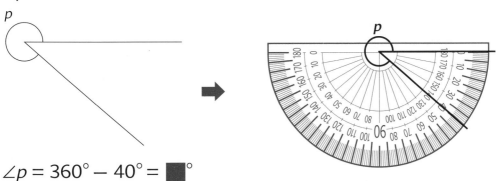

∠p = 360° − 40° = ◼°

7. What is the size of each marked angle?

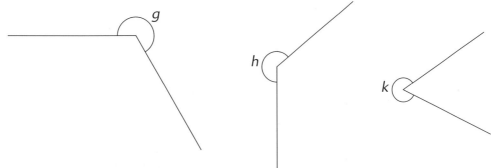

8. Draw an angle equal to 200°.

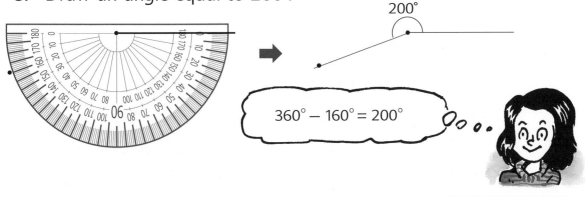

200°

360° − 160° = 200°

Workbook Exercise 43

9. In the figure, ABCD is a rectangle and ∠DAC = 26°.
   Find ∠BAC.

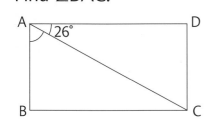

∠BAD = 90°

Workbook Exercise 44

Perpendicular and Parallel Lines

1 Perpendicular Lines

These are examples of **perpendicular lines**.

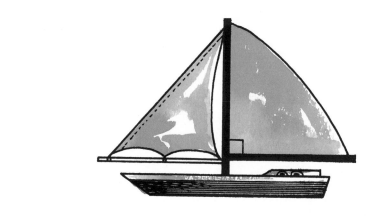

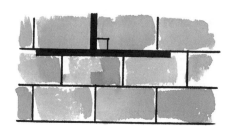

We mark a right angle to show perpendicular lines.

Look for some more examples of perpendicular lines around you.

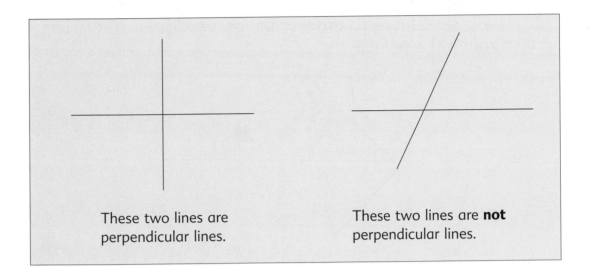

These two lines are perpendicular lines.

These two lines are **not** perpendicular lines.

We can use a set-square to check perpendicular lines.

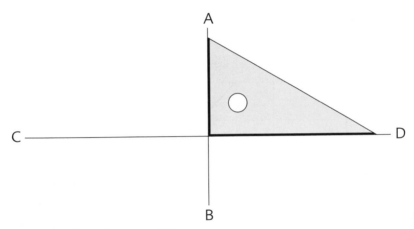

AB is perpendicular to CD.
We write: **AB ⊥ CD**

1. How many pairs of perpendicular lines are there in each figure?
   Name each pair of perpendicular lines.

(a)

(b)

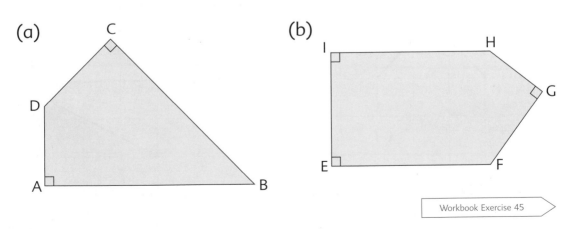

Workbook Exercise 45

2. Use a set-square to draw a line perpendicular to the line AB through the point P.

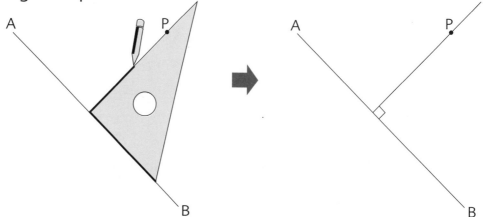

3. Here are some examples of perpendicular lines drawn on a square grid.
   Find out how they are drawn.

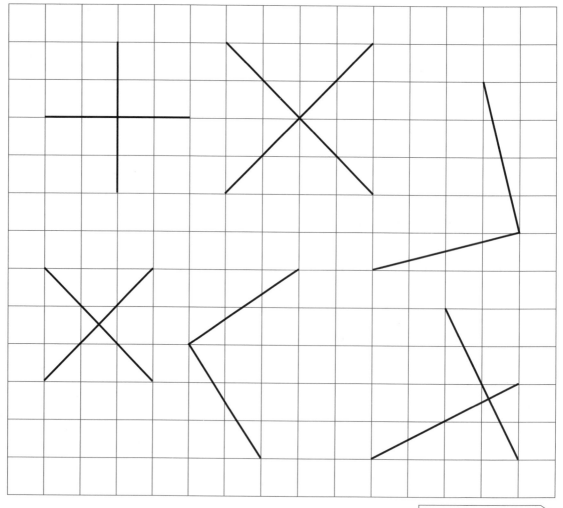

Workbook Exercise 46

② Parallel Lines

These are examples of **parallel lines**.

We draw arrowheads to show parallel lines.

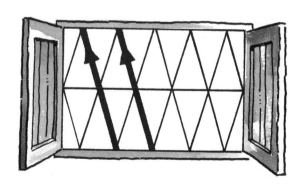

Look for some more examples of parallel lines around you.

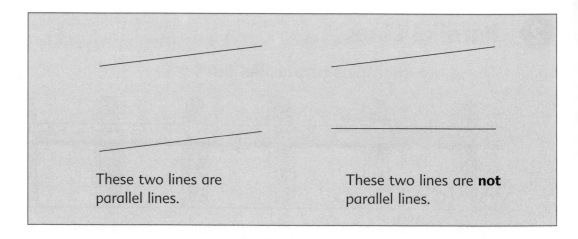

These two lines are parallel lines.

These two lines are **not** parallel lines.

We can slide a set-square along a ruler to check parallel lines.

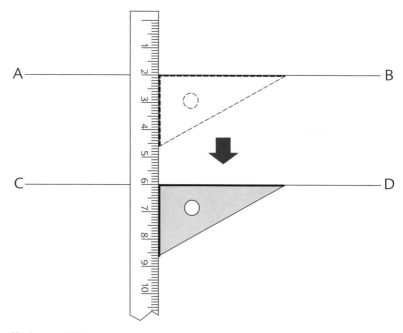

AB is parallel to CD.
We write: **AB // CD**

1. In the 5-sided figure PQRST, which two sides are perpendicular to each other?
   Which two sides are parallel to each other?

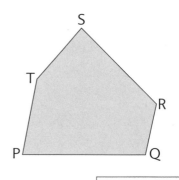

Workbook Exercise 47

82

2. Use a set-square and a ruler to draw a line parallel to the line AB through the point P.

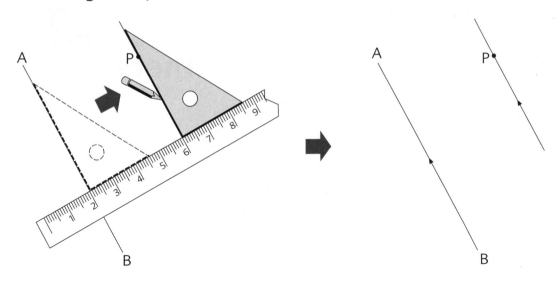

3. Here are some examples of parallel lines drawn on a square grid. Find out how they are drawn.

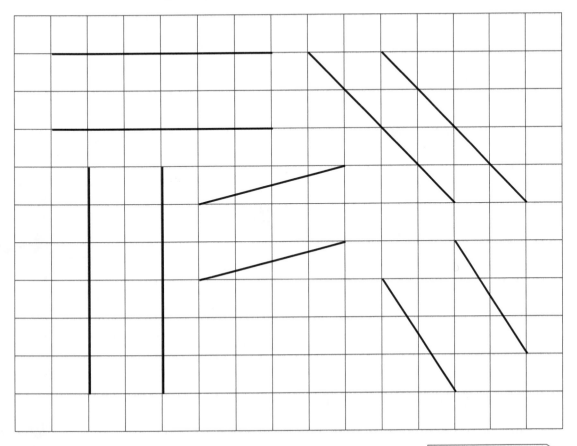

Workbook Exercise 48

Area and Perimeter

1 Rectangles and Squares

The rectangle measures 9 cm by 5 cm.
Find its area and perimeter.

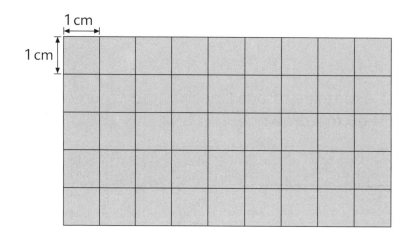

$9 \times 5 =$ ■

Area of rectangle
= Length × Width

The area of the rectangle is ■ cm^2.

Perimeter of rectangle
= Total length of 4 sides

$9 + 5 + 9 + 5 =$ ■

The perimeter of the rectangle is ■ cm.

1. The perimeter of a rectangle is 24 m.
   If the length of the rectangle is 8 m, find its width.

   Total length of 4 sides = 24 m

   Length + Width

   = 24 ÷ 2 = 12 m

   Length = 8 m

   Width = 12 − 8 = ■ m

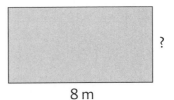

?

8 m

2. The rectangle and the square have the same perimeter.
   (a) Find the length of the rectangle.
   (b) Which has a bigger area, the rectangle or the square?

5 cm

?

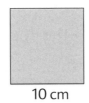

10 cm

3. The perimeter of a square is 20 m.
   Find its area.

   Length of one side = 20 ÷ 4

   = ■ m

   Area of square   = ■ m²

?

Find the length of
one side first.

4. The area of a square is 36 cm². Find its perimeter.

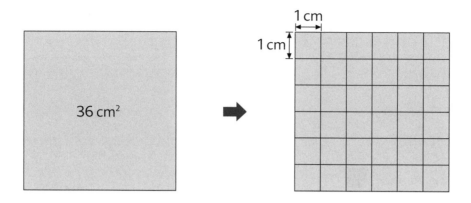

$36 = 6 \times 6$

Length of one side = 6 cm

Perimeter of square = ■ cm

5. The area of a rectangle is 40 m². If the length of the rectangle is 8 m, find its width and perimeter.

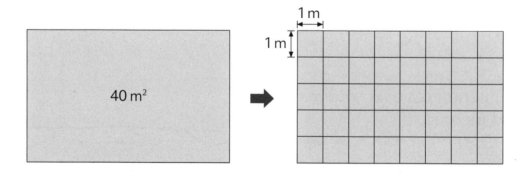

$40 = 8 \times 5$

Length = 8 m

Width = ■ m

Perimeter = ■ m

Workbook Exercise 49

2 Composite Figures

Each of the following figures is made up of two rectangles.
Find the area and perimeter of each figure.

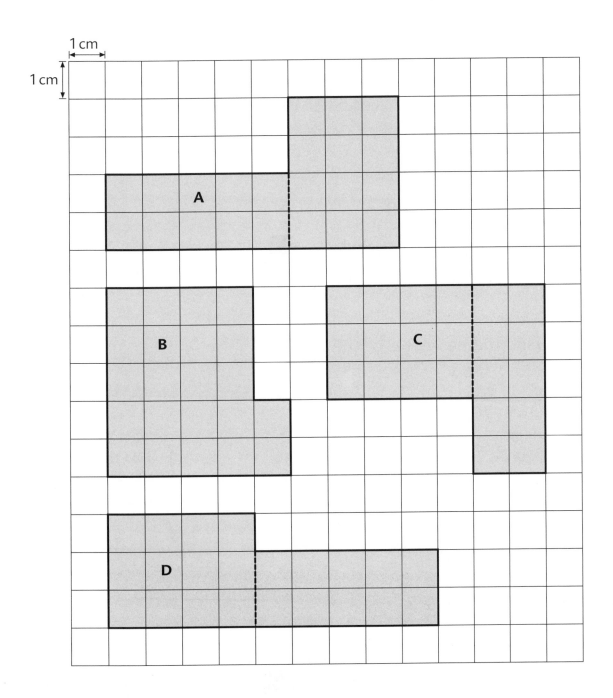

Do the figures have the same area?
Do they have the same perimeter?

1. Find the perimeter of the figure.

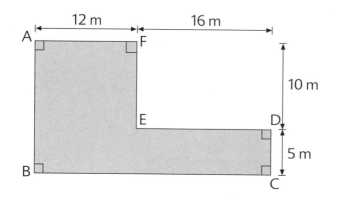

Find the lengths of AB and BC first.

AB = 10 + 5 = 15 m

BC = 12 + 16 = 28 m

12 + 10 + 16 + 5 + 28 + 15 = ■

The perimeter of the figure is ■ m.

2. Find the perimeter of the figure.

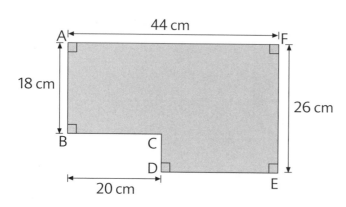

Find the lengths of CD and DE first.

CD = 26 − 18 = 8 cm

DE = 44 − 20 = 24 cm

44 + 26 + 24 + 8 + 20 + 18 = ■

The perimeter of the figure is ■ cm.

Workbook Exercise 50

3. The figure is made up of two rectangles.
   Find its area.

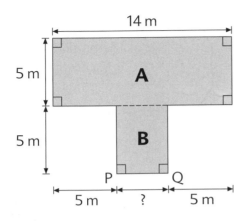 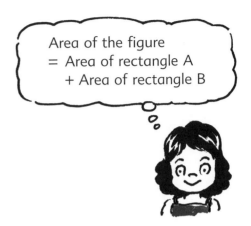

Area of the figure
= Area of rectangle A
    + Area of rectangle B

Area of rectangle A = $14 \times 5 = 70$ m^2
PQ = $14 - 5 - 5 = 4$ m
Area of rectangle B = $4 \times 5 = 20$ m^2
Total area = ■ m^2

4. The figure shows a small rectangle in a big rectangle.
   Find the area of the shaded part of the big rectangle.

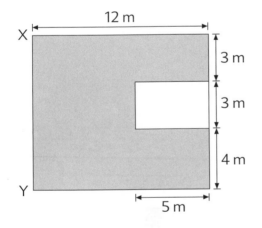 

Area of shaded part
= Area of big rectangle
    − Area of small rectangle

XY = $3 + 3 + 4 = 10$ m
Area of big rectangle = $12 \times 10 = 120$ m^2
Area of small rectangle = $5 \times 3 = 15$ m^2

Area of shaded part = ■ m^2

Workbook Exercise 51

5. The figure shows a rectangular field with a path 1 m wide around it.
    Find the area of the path.

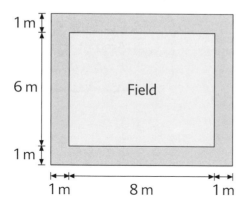

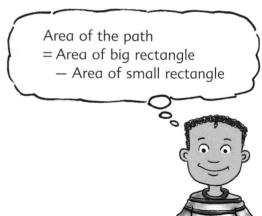

Area of the path
= Area of big rectangle
    − Area of small rectangle

Length of big rectangle = 8 + 1 + 1 = 10 m

Width of big rectangle = 6 + 1 + 1 = 8 m

Area of big rectangle   = 10 × 8 = ■ m²

Area of small rectangle = ■ m²

Area of the path   = ■ m²

6. The figure shows a small rectangle in a big rectangle.
    Find the area of the shaded part of the big rectangle.

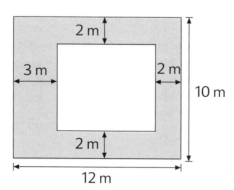

Area of big rectangle   = 12 × 10 = ■ m²

Length of small rectangle = ■ m

Width of small rectangle   = ■ m

Area of small rectangle   = ■ m²

Area of shaded part   = ■ m²

Workbook Exercise 52

PRACTICE 7A

1. Find the unknown side and the area of each of the following rectangles.

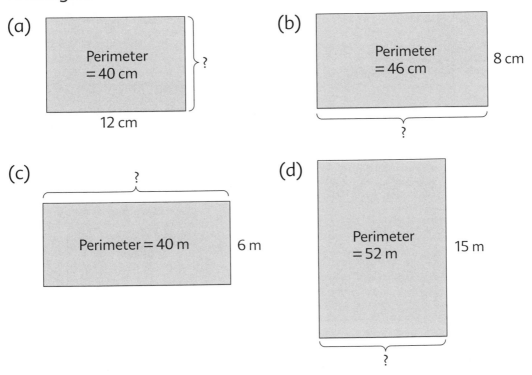

(a) Perimeter = 40 cm, 12 cm, ?

(b) Perimeter = 46 cm, 8 cm, ?

(c) ?, Perimeter = 40 m, 6 m

(d) Perimeter = 52 m, 15 m, ?

2. Find the unknown side and the perimeter of each of the following rectangles.

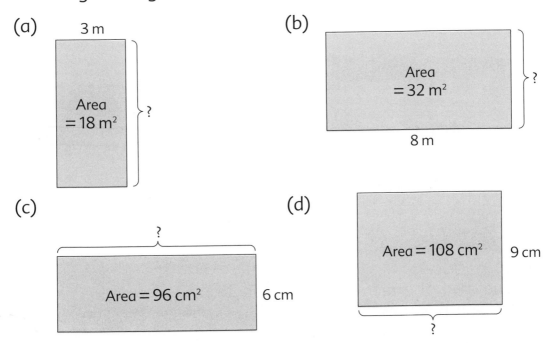

(a) 3 m, Area = 18 m², ?

(b) Area = 32 m², ?, 8 m

(c) ?, Area = 96 cm², 6 cm

(d) Area = 108 cm², 9 cm, ?

3. Find the area and perimeter of each figure. (All lines meet at right angles.)

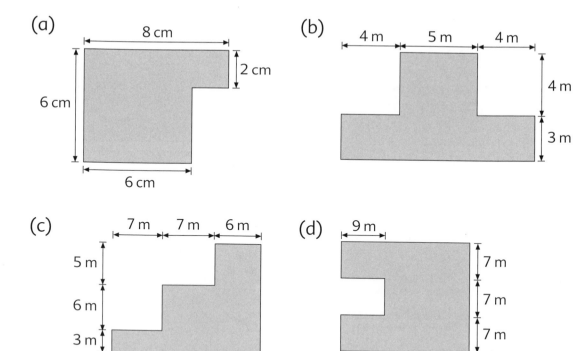

(a)
8 cm
2 cm
6 cm
6 cm

(b)
4 m   5 m   4 m
4 m
3 m

(c)
7 m   7 m   6 m
5 m
6 m
3 m

(d)
9 m
7 m
7 m
7 m
26 m

4. Each of the following figures shows a small rectangle in a big rectangle.
Find the area of the shaded part of each rectangle.

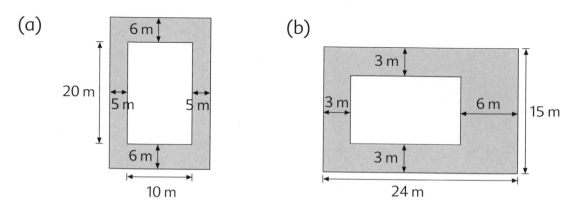

(a)
6 m
20 m
5 m   5 m
6 m
10 m

(b)
3 m
3 m   6 m   15 m
3 m
24 m

5. The area of a rectangular wall is 36 m².
Its length is 9 m.
Find the height of the wall.

6. The border around a square painting is 4 cm wide.
   Each side of the painting is 40 cm long.
   Find the area of the border.

4 cm   40 cm   4 cm

7. A rectangular flower-bed measures 10 m by 6 m.
   It has a path 2 m wide around it.
   Find the area of the path.

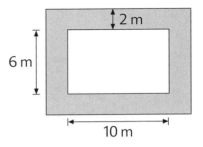

6 m

2 m

10 m

8. A rectangular piece of glass measures 60 cm by 46 cm.
   When it is placed on a table, it leaves a margin 4 cm wide all
   round it.
   What is the area of the table-top **not** covered by the glass?

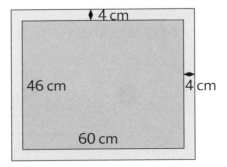

4 cm

46 cm

4 cm

60 cm

9. A rectangular piece of carpet is placed
   on the floor of a room which measures
   8 m by 7 m.
   It leaves a margin 1 m wide around it.
   Find the area of the carpet.

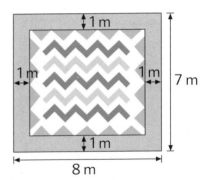

1 m

1 m   1 m   7 m

1 m

8 m

REVIEW C

1. Estimate and then multiply.
    (a) 39×19 (b) 48×22 (c) 99×4
    (d) 208×31 (e) 512×28 (f) 198×6

2. The product of two numbers is 108.
    If one of the numbers is 6, what is the other number?

3. Name 3 equivalent fractions for each of these fractions.

    (a) $\dfrac{2}{3}$ (b) $\dfrac{1}{5}$ (c) $\dfrac{9}{12}$

4. Arrange the numbers in increasing order.

    (a) $\dfrac{3}{4}$, $\dfrac{2}{3}$, $\dfrac{5}{6}$ (b) $\dfrac{7}{4}$, $1\dfrac{7}{10}$, 2

5. Write each fraction in its simplest form.

    (a) $\dfrac{6}{8}$ (b) $\dfrac{18}{24}$ (c) $\dfrac{20}{50}$

6. Write **>** (is greater than), **<** (is less than), or **=** (is equal to) in place
    of each ■.

    (a) $\dfrac{9}{10}$ ■ $\dfrac{3}{4}$ (b) $1\dfrac{1}{4}$ ■ $\dfrac{10}{8}$ (c) $1\dfrac{2}{3}$ ■ $\dfrac{3}{2}$

7. Find the length and perimeter of the rectangle.

    Area = 78 m²   6 m

    ?

8. The perimeter of a square is 48 cm.
    Find its area.

9. Each of the following figures shows a small rectangle in a big rectangle.
   Find the area of the shaded part of each figure.

(a)

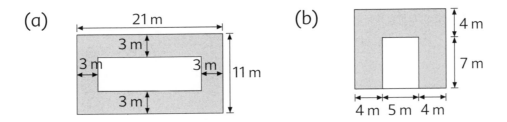

(b)

10. Find the perimeter and area of each figure. (All lines meet at right angles.)

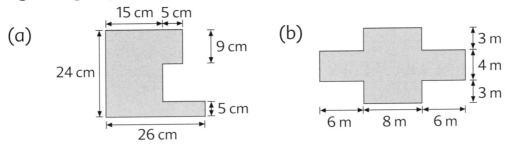

(a)

(b)

11.

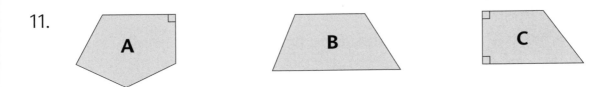

(a) Which figures have perpendicular lines?
(b) Which figures have parallel lines?
(c) Which figure has both perpendicular and parallel lines?

12. Which of the following figures have 4 right angles?
    Which is a square?

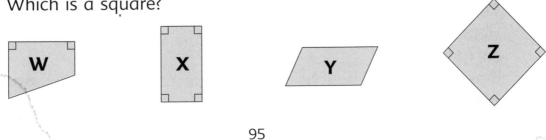

13. The table shows the number of people who attended four courses in a community center.
Draw a bar graph to show the data given in the table.

Course	Number of People
Cooking	27
Art	25
Computer	49
Dancing	30

14. Make a table to show the following data.

Kevin
Height : 154 cm
Weight : 41 kg
Age: 11 yr 2 mth

Travis
Height : 153 cm
Weight : 44 kg
Age: 11 yr 10 mth

Seth
Height : 160 cm
Weight : 48 kg
Age: 13 yr 8 mth

15. Seth used $4\frac{2}{5}$ yd of rope to pitch a tent.

Roger used $\frac{3}{10}$ yd less rope to pitch another tent.
How many yards of rope did they use altogether?

16. Twelve pieces of ribbon, each 75 in. long, are cut from a length of ribbon 1250 in. long.
What is the length of the remaining piece of ribbon?

17. 45 people took part in a swimming competition.
The number of people who took part in a walkathon was 12 times the number of people who took part in the swimming competition.
How many more people took part in the walkathon than in the swimming competition?

18. Rolando imported 138 boxes of mangoes.
There were 24 mangoes in each box.
He reserved 72 mangoes for his friends and sold the rest to 3 customers.
If each customer bought an equal number of mangoes, how many mangoes did each customer buy?